Also by Kim Klaver (aka Ms. Stud)

Books

Rules for the New New MLMer. 2000. For someone who wants better than 'The 5 worst things to say to a good prospect' and who's ready to learn much more savvy and intriguing things to draw out the best and the brightest.

The Truth. What it really rakes to make it in Network Marketing. 1999. A 200-page full color giant cartoon book with 14 reaching out methods laid out in fun detail.

Audios

So you want to be a networker? A single audio which gives a humorous introduction to what it takes to make it in the networking business. 1996

How to Build a Giant Heap with or without your friends, family or neighbors. 2-tape set, for people doing the business. 1997

How to be an awesome sponsor and keep your heap. A single audio which shows people how to keep the ones they want to keep. 1998

Survival Skills For The Advanced Heap Builder. Single audio for those who want ways to get good people to listen. 2000

Websites

http://www.maxout.com or http://www.mlm911.com

Everything available at http://www.mlm911.com or 800.595.1956

Max Out Productions, Inc.
http://www.maxout.com

Virtually in every corner of the world™ ☺

DO YOU
HAVE A

Plan

B?

Guide to an Alternative Career in
Direct Sales and network Marketing

Kim Klaver

Max Out Productions
4741 Central Street, #300
Kansas City, MO 64112
816.333.6619
Visit our website at http://www.maxout.com

ISBN # 1-891493-10-8

Klaver, Kim
Do You Have a Plan B?/Kim Klaver

Printed in the United States of America
First Printing

Go on and live your life as it is. It's a good life. You don't need this. I don't believe in being interested in subjects because it's said to be important and interesting.

I believe in being caught by it somehow or other.

But you may find that with the proper introduction this subject will catch you.

And so, what can it do for you when it DOES catch you?

Joseph Campbell
The Power of Myth with Bill Moyers

After all, what if it does work?™☺

Acknowledgements

I am indebted to my many students and friends who, over the last six years, have shared with me their trials and successes in direct sales and network marketing. And especially the thousands who participate on my twice-a-week international conference calls, and the hundreds of people I have come to know through the 6-week intensive Max Out Productions Blitz training programs. I am certain that I have learned more from you than you have from me.

I also wish to gratefully acknowledge good friends and professionals who have given their time to reviews of earlier drafts. In alpha order, my readers, each of whom made significant improvements to the original work, were Heidi C. Dulay, Paula English, Jacqueline Freeman, Dan Hollings, Maria Hyman and Vicki Link. You have made this a much better book than it was in the beginning. Thank you.

TABLE OF CONTENTS

TABLE OF CONTENTS

TABLE OF CONTENTS

1.
Do You Have a Plan B?

A Plan B? You know, that back-up plan in case whatever you're doing now, doesn't pan out?

No, not a stash in the mattress, or the disability insurance plan. Not Social Security, either, which many people hope will kick in to take care of them during retirement years.

This is the other plan B.

Perhaps it's your secret dream. The thing you've always promised yourself you'd start someday.

Or it might be the Plan B you suddenly need to create 'out of thin air' because something drastic and unexpected happened to your Plan A.

Or perhaps you wake up one day and decide that you've had it with the way things are in your life.

Maybe you've had it with work relationships or stresses that you decide right now are no longer worth it.

Perhaps you've discovered that you do not take direction from others well after all.

Or you suddenly realize you forgot to plan for your retirement.

Or you meet up with an old classmate you haven't seen in ten years, who golfs every afternoon. He says it's because he has something of his own now. An alternative career. A Plan B.

Hmm.

How do people do that? How do they start if they've never done anything on their own before? And how do they do it so there's a good chance of success?

You know, in your lifetime?

2.
Careers: Alternative and Mainstream

So what's an alternative career?

Hmm. 'Alternative' first. Here's from American Heritage:

al · ter · na · tive[1]
adj

    a.   Existing outside traditional or established institutions or systems: *an alternative lifestyle.*

    b.   Espousing or reflecting values that are different from those of the

---

[1] *The American Heritage® Dictionary of the English Language, Fourth Edition (2000),* www.dictionary.com.

establishment or mainstream: *an alternative newspaper; alternative greeting cards.*

And here's the *career* part:

ca·reer[2]
n.

A chosen pursuit; a profession or occupation.

So an *alternative career* is a career outside the mainstream.

It's a 'chosen pursuit' that reflects 'values that are different from those of the establishment or mainstream'.

How about mainstream, then?

A mainstream career is any regular job[3].

---

[2] ibid, www.dictionary.com

[3] **job** *n.* 1.   A regular activity performed in exchange for payment, especially as one's trade, occupation, or profession. 2.   A position in which one is employed.

A job is that thing most Americans do and are taught to do in our schools, to earn their living.

The President of the United States holds a job. The Pope holds a job. In any company, from the president on down, everyone is an employee, be the company large or small. As long as they get a regular paycheck, that's what they are.

Remember, jobs are positioned and promoted early - even in kindergarten - as that thing good people do when they grow up. Jobs comprise a very big and necessary part of the American economy.

Some 133,976 million Americans hold jobs. [4] Ambitious people hold more than one. You know, so they can live where they want and have what they want. (Especially if they live in California or New York!)

For most people, jobs are the right thing to be doing. Good match. That's why it's mainstream.

---

[4] As of April 2002, according to the U.S. Bureau of Labor Statistics, Washington, D.C., (202) 691-5200

And then there are the others, of whom you may be one, seeking a Plan B. Something totally different. Something of your own. Something in the alternative zone.

3.
Do You Have an Inner Entrepreneur?

You'll need it to pull off a Plan B. Here are three ways to recognize if you have it.

1. Your inner entrepreneur (E) has been out since you were a kid

Are you obsessed by something? Do you feel 'called' to a special cause or 'thing'? Is there something you just cannot get out of your mind? Does it feel good just to think about it, do it, or experience it? Are you doing it already?

Sometimes that special passion catches someone already in childhood and the inner entrepreneur pops out early.

That's what happened to Estée Lauder, the cosmetics mogul. When she was a little girl, she

"...enjoyed experimenting with her mother's skin creams and fragrances. But Esty's interest in beauty products and other symbols of femininity extended beyond trying them on herself. From her earliest days, she wanted to alter other people's appearance, to pat cream onto their faces, brush their hair, and apply lip rouge (lipstick). Esty started at home, applying what she called 'treatments' to her family members and friends."[5]

Like so many entrepreneurs, her parents were not enthused.

"[Her father] admonished his daughter to stop 'fiddling with other people's faces'."[6]

"But," writes the author, little Esty "could not obey her father. She was obsessed with the possibilities that cosmetics afforded women."[7]

---

[5] Nancy Koehn (2001), p. 150

[6] ibid p. 150

[7] ibid, p. 151

She was infatuated with her Plan B from the first, and did it despite her parents' objections, just like Michael Dell, H.J. Heinz and others did. That's one reason you need that inner entrepreneur. To help overcome such obstacles.

2. **As an adult you yearn for something of your own.**

Some folks are driven by an inner desire to create something of their own. They're filled with ideas and want to change their lives so they get to work on THEIR projects, not someone else's.

Steve Jobs, for example, co-founded Apple Computer as an adult, and then, within ten years, set up a second computer/software venture, called NEXT.

Today, he oversees that AND a third venture, Pixar. You've probably seen his work even. Pixar does the animation for movies like *Toy Story*. Now there's a driven entrepreneur with multiple streams of income - multiple Plan Bs.

There's no limit on how many Plan Bs one might pursue. It just depends on your time, energy and how many good partners you can attract.

Are you perhaps in the middle of doing your Plan A right now, but you regularly get that little voice telling you that you need to be doing something else? That your Plan A is NOT what YOU really want?

Perhaps someone else wanted that Plan A for you, (mom, dad, spouse, boss) but now you realize Plan A doesn't ring your bell.

Or might you just need more income to do those other things you want to do and Plan A isn't cutting it?

Your inner entrepreneur may be ready for action.

3. A desperate situation pushes you to consider a Plan B

Perhaps your Plan A just disappeared. Did your company go under unexpectedly? Are you being threatened by layoffs? Think Enron, Andersen.

CBS.MarketWatch.com reports that payrolls dropped by 1.2 million in 22 months. After 9/11 U.S. job cuts in 2001 approached the 2 million mark. As examples here is a partial list of employment reductions.

In Technology, 519,000 jobs; the Airlines, 91,000; Retail layoffs at 82,000; and Manufacturing at 367,000; Financial industry reports 93,000 jobs lost; and the Media, 15,000; the Internet, 16,000 jobs; and Miscellaneous industries at 40,000 layoffs. This is an unbelievable total of approximately 1.2 million layoffs, and this is only a partial list.[8]

---

[8] http://cbs.marketwatch.com/news/economy/layoffs.asp?sit eid=mktw

Are you now ready to find or create something that has a future you can control on your terms?

This is your inner entrepreneur speaking.

If any of these three scenarios describe you, and you are ready to make that change, you're ready to see if you've got what it takes for an alternative career in direct sales and network marketing.

First, some tidbits about entrepreneurs you may want to know up front.

4.
What You May Not Know about Entrepreneurs

Three little-known facts that are helpful whether you are (becoming) one or live with one.
(E = entrepreneur)

1. They wear E-colored glasses
2. They may be late bloomers
3. The U.S. President and Government love them

1. E-colored glasses

When someone decides to follow their E-flame, you may be surprised to notice that suddenly these folks take on a different view of certain things out there. It's as though they've magically put on a pair of E-colored glasses through which they now see parts of their world.

For example, a task they perceived as risky before, or even scary, has inexplicably become a challenge.

An old 'too hard' task now creates an adrenalin rush that spurs them to action. Fear? What fear?

This new attitude may be just for their 'thing', however. It may not be visible in other areas of their life. (For those entrepreneurs that have an 'other area' of their life. Ha-ha.)

At those other times, they're in their regular Plan A mode. With just regular, maintenance-mode juices flowing. This is not lost on those around them.

Ask anyone who lives with one. They'll tell you that the E-flame doesn't appear in their entrepreneurial mate for, say, cleaning up their room. Or painting the garage. Or housework. But they'll stay up all night writing, tinkering, planning or doing their 'thing'.

Sometimes this distinction starts early. Here's the story of Henry Heinz, whose name everyone associates with ketchup.

Henry J. Heinz. When Henry was 12 years old, (in the 1860s) the lad was already an avid farmer and gardener. His biographer, Nancy Koehn, describes him:

"Before and after school hours, Henry helped in his father's brickyard. He also led horses along the canal's towpath and dug potatoes for a neighboring farmer, earning twenty-five cents a day and meals for his time. He loved virtually all farming activities. From an early age, he had helped his mother in the family garden, first tending it and later selling its surplus to local grocers. Among a community of meticulous gardeners, the Heinz plot was known for its clean, straight rows, varied produce, and consistent bounty. Fascinated by the effects of weather, soil, light and the farmer's efforts on the final harvest, Henry was a talented gardener and a gifted salesman. By the time he was twelve, he had his own personal plot, a horse, a cart, and a growing list of customers."[9]

Obviously he was caught up by these activities.

When Henry finished school at fourteen, he enrolled in a seminary at the behest of his mother, who had hoped Henry would go into the ministry. Here is, in a nutshell, what the school authorities said about him during his short stint:

"He was not an exceptional student or a particularly reflective young man. He found it difficult to sit still, and his exuberance for work, especially that involving physical activity did not extend to reading."[10]

So, "before long," writes his biographer, "Henry left the seminary, ending his family's hopes for his career in the church."[11]

---

[9] Nancy Koehn (2001), p. 51

[10] ibid, p. 51

[11] ibid, p. 51

Obviously, his reflection skills and energy were selectively applied to what he loved.

It's just that his "exuberance did NOT extend to say, learning to sit still, or to reading."[12] Same thing happened to Thomas Edison in second grade. (And countless others.)

Those E-colored glasses were on early.

Now, what if you're older? You know, older than 26? Or 56? Or 76?

Is it ever too late to fan the E-flame?

2. Late Bloomers

While some people get 'caught up' in their fantasies and urgings pretty early in life, (Edison, Heinz, Rockefeller, Estée Lauder, Dell, Gates) others get that chance later. Perhaps they weren't ready earlier, or they just 'found' their Plan B later. Or

---

[12] ibid, p. 53

they've finally became too desperate to stay with Plan A any longer. Here are three late bloomers.

Over 40. Mary Kay Ash. "After a lengthy and successful career in direct sales, Mary Kay Ash retired in 1963 for a month. During those four weeks, she decided to write a book to help women thrive in the male-dominated business world. Sitting at her kitchen table, she made two lists: one contained the good things she had seen in companies for which she had worked, the other featured things she thought could be improved.

"When she reviewed the lists, she realized that she had inadvertently created a marketing plan for a successful 'dream company.' With her life savings of $5,000 and the help of her 20-year-old son Richard Rogers, she launched Mary Kay Cosmetics on Friday, September 13, 1963." She was 45 years old. In 2000 Mary Kay Cosmetics, revenues listed at $1.2 billion.[13]

---

[13] http://www.marykaytribute.com/HerLife1.htm
http://www.marykay.com/home/community/Headquarters/
MaryKayBiography/Biography/Page3/Page3.asp

Over 50. Ray Kroc. Ray Kroc founded the great McDonald's enterprise after he had been a salesman for over 30 years.

For three decades before that, Ray Kroc had been an energized, innovative but financially unsuccessful restaurant supply salesman. He met the McDonald brothers in 1954 when he sold them their Multimixer to use in their little hamburger store in San Bernardino, CA.

The opportunity that was to change the world came later in his life. And that's not all.

Kroc was also DESPERATE. That's why he grabbed at a financially dreadful deal when he first agreed to head up the brothers' national franchise operation. Kroc's biographer writes about this period:

"That Kroc accepted the [franchising] deal was the surest evidence of his desperation. 'I went along with it because the Multimixer business was so bad, and I had to get into something that had a future,' Kroc recalled."[14]

A late bloomer, that Ray Kroc. And a desperado as well at the time he happened across his major opportunity and turned the world in a new direction with it.

Over 60. Colonel Harland Sanders. And then we have the story of Kentucky Fried Chicken's Colonel Harland Sanders, who started his empire at age 65 and a monthly Social Security check of $105.

Early on, Colonel Sanders had a small restaurant seating 142 people in Corbin, Kentucky where he served his chicken to a loyal following and "over nine years perfected his select brand of 11 herbs and spices and the basic cooking technique that is still in use today."[15] His fame grew and he was made a Kentucky Colonel in 1935 by Governor Ruby Laffoon.

---

[14] John Love (1986), p. 41

[15] http://www/kfc.com/about/story.htm

In the early 1950's a new interstate highway was built bypassing the town of Corbin. The colonel saw the end of his business, auctioned off his operation, and after paying the bills was left to living on his monthly Social Security check of $105.

Kentucky Fried Chicken was born.

"Confident of the quality of his fried chicken, the Colonel devoted himself to the chicken franchising business that he started in 1952. He traveled across the country by car from restaurant to restaurant, cooking batches of chicken for restaurant owners and their employees. If the reaction was favorable, he entered into a handshake agreement on a deal that stipulated a payment to him of a nickel for each chicken the restaurant sold. By 1964, Colonel Sanders had more than 600 franchised outlets for his chicken in the United States and Canada. That year, he sold his interest in the U.S. company for $2 million to a group of investors... The Colonel remained a public spokesman for the company. In 1976, an independent survey ranked the Colonel as the world's second most recognizable celebrity.[16]

Although the company went public and changed hands a couple of times and was finally acquired by PepsiCo for $840 million, the Colonel traveled 250,000 miles a year visiting the KFC empire he founded until he was 90. (!)

Evidently, the adage "When the student is ready the teacher will appear" is true also for the entrepreneurial flame. It seems it is never too late, nor to soon, for it to show itself. Being desperate helps because it makes people consider options they wouldn't look at if their lives were more comfortable.

3. The U.S. President and the Federal Government recognize Es with Plan Bs

Some people don't realize this. In his world-televised comments March 9, 2002 President Bush introduced the economic stimulus package he

---

[16] ibid

planned to sign as "...a piece of good news for workers and entrepreneurs..."

Hmm. Workers. Entrepreneurs.

Workers first because there are so many more of them. Yet without entrepreneurs to start a Plan B that could grow, what would mainstream workers do?

Bush and the members of Congress specifically recognized the two groups in creating the legislation, so the economic stimulus package they created, and which Bush signed, has provisions to 'stimulate' both groups to carry on with what they're doing.

This is a very good thing. Many government incentives encourage entrepreneurs to try their Plan Bs. Tax advantages, for example.[17]

---

[17] Kevin Wilkes http://www.taxhelper.com/g.o/tax A tax application like Quicken, but for mlm. And Eva Rosenburg's free e-newsletter. http://www.taxmama.com/subscribe

The country needs both mainstream workers and entrepreneurs with their Plan B's.

So what is direct sales and network marketing, and how have entrepreneurs used this as an effective Plan B? Direct sales first.

5.
Direct Sales Is...

Here's from the Direct Selling Organization, the body representing the direct sales industry:

"Direct Selling refers to the marketing of consumer products directly to consumers, generally in their homes or the homes of others, at their workplace and other places **away from a permanent retail location**, usually through explanation or demonstration of the products by a direct seller."[18]

The DSA adds:

"These products and services are marketed to customers by independent salespeople. Depending on the company, the salespeople may be called

---

[18] From the Direct Selling Association (DSA) World code. http://www.dsa.ca/ethics.html#Definitions . Emphasis added.

distributors, representatives, consultants or various other titles."[19]

So we can say that a direct seller is "...any individual engaged on his/her own behalf or on behalf of an active [direct selling company], selling products through personal sales contacts, which may also include contacts via telemarketing and/or direct mail..."[20]

Direct sales can be used to market one's own creations, or those of someone else. As in products and services 'on behalf of an active direct selling company'.

Why do people use direct sales to get their products or services out?

One reason: Sometimes **the mainstream isn't ready to receive them yet**. Some new or alternative products or services might be for just

---

[19] From the US DSA http://www.dsa.org/selling/selling.htm

[20] Direct Selling Association (DSA) World code (2002), http://www.edge-interactive.com/dsa/code.html#definitions

the courageous, or independent minded trendsetters, at least at first.

Estée Lauder. She did direct sales on her own behalf, since she had created some novel make-up products in her kitchen that were not available anywhere. So how would her prospective customers ever find out about her wonderful stuff if someone didn't SHOW it to them? So they could experience the wonder of it?

Especially considering that her product line was risqué at the time she introduced it.

Opposition to the use of cosmetics in years past was very big in some circles, and continued into the 19th century.

"Many early Christian writers opposed the use of makeup and hair color regarding these practices as deceitful or wanton. Powdering one's face or 'laying blush on the cheeks' altered God's creation and must be the work of the Devil, declared St. Cyprian, the 3rd century bishop.   Writing a century later, St. Ambrose was more virulent: 'Oh woman,' he wrote, 'thou defacest the picture if thou daubest thy countenance with material whitenesse or a borrowed red...Do not take away God's picturing and assume the picture of a harlot.'"[21]

That's why, the author says, cosmetics queens Estée Lauder, Helena Rubenstein and Madame Celeste J. Walker, in the early 1900s, could not go mainstream. So instead, they did direct sales.

"[They] worked outside the established wholesale and retailing systems, distributing their products by mail order, direct through the growing number of beauty salons and door-to-door."[22]

Word of mouth did the rest of the work. People could SEE it and FEEL it. And their friends said, "Gosh, you look wonderful. What did you do?" And you know the rest.

---

[21] Nancy F. Koehn (2001), p. 144

[22] ibid, p. 146

A product line doesn't have to be risqué to use the direct sales model. Another reason people use direct sales is that **for certain types of products that require explanation, education, demonstration, or personal attention, direct sales is a smarter way to market.**

Michael Dell. Here's what happened when IBM launched its first PC in 1982.

"IBM received thousands of phone calls from business consumers and (retail) distributors... because the retailers from whom they had purchased the computers provided little or no help. Frustrated dealers themselves contacted IBM to learn how to respond to the queries they were receiving from consumers."[23]

What chaos!

A young entrepreneur named Michael Dell "perceived a huge opportunity in **how** PCs were sold." He saw that business consumers "...cared

---

[23] ibid, p.277

about more than price and computing power. They also wanted knowledgeable, responsive service, after-sales support, and a say in how their machines were configured to meet specific needs. In 1983, few manufacturers or retailers were providing these benefits to small and medium-sized companies."[24]

Ms. Koehn, a Dell biographer, then states that young Dell concluded that

"...a business organized around direct sales, customer input, and product support, could fill a significant opening in the market."

"This," she says, "turned out to be the key business vision of Dell's career."[25]

Dell's business model in the 1980s was therefore "based on personal interaction with consumers. The vast majority of the firm's customers were

---

[24] ibid, p. 277

[25] ibid, p. 277

reached by phone."[26]. The Dell salespeople would find out how a computer might help that company, what they needed it to do, etc.

Dell saw that the strategy of retail stores marketing the computers to customers "was based on a marriage of the unknowing buyers and the unknowledgeable seller." He was sure, says Ms. Koehn, that such a marriage could not last.[27]

Dell on the other hand, communicated with consumers more effectively because of how he sold his computers – direct to the customers. NOT through stores. Consumers needed education and support about the computers they were buying, and Dell's direct sales approach was the only one that offered customers that.

Dell's key entrepreneurial vision was his realization that:

---

[26] ibid, p. 281

[27] ibid, p.280

"HOW a new product such as the PC was presented, sold, and serviced to consumers was just as critical as how it was made, and he used this insight to build **strong, direct connections with customers.** These connections were invaluable in helping Dell anticipate what buyers wanted and how to earn their loyalty...these relationships with consumers became the bedrock of his product offerings, operating strategy, and brand."[28]

"By the early 21st century, Dell Computer's business model...had become the industry standard. Millions of business and home users around the world associated the Dell brand with quality information technology (IT) products, direct sales, customer control, and responsive service and support."[29]

This then is how direct sales works.

---

[28] ibid, p. 261
[29] ibid, p. 261

The role of the direct seller is to introduce and educate people about products and services that are new, different, innovative, or alternative, and which are best demonstrated or experienced by customers.

These days, alternative medical treatment options, nutritional and wellness products, and even telecom services, are products that require introduction and education. If such innovative products and services are in stores at all, it's mostly the blind leading the blind, and buyers don't get the education and personal attention they need to make the best used of their purchases. Who needs that?

Here's how the money works in direct sales and network marketing.

6.
Show Me the Money

In direct sales and network marketing, people are paid commissions from the direct sales they make. There is no 'salary' or 'regular check'.

That's one reason it's an alternative career. People who choose this option believe they can make more with a 100% commission position than they could ever earn on a regular salary, given the same time and effort put in.

Here are two ways the money comes in. Since network marketers do direct sales of products and services, we'll cover the money for that first.

Commissions off the bottom

Entrepreneurs like Estée Lauder and Michael Dell earned their income through direct sales of their products. They got whatever was left of the sales after they paid all their expenses (cost of make-up, computer parts, research and development efforts, etc.), because they created the products and services they sold.

When someone creates their own product or service, and they market through direct sales, they get whatever's left after paying the costs of creating and marketing their goods. That's why it's called 'commissions off the bottom'. It may take a while before there's anything left for the entrepreneur to pick up, but for Estee and Michael, they were in the money within their first few years. Others take longer. And some never get into the money.

Commissions off the top

People in direct sales and network marketing introduce others to products, services or 'properties' that were created by or are serviced by others. These folks get their commissions off the top. Their cut is a percent of the selling price of the product or service. Those who have the product to sell in the first place are the ones who pay it to them.

Would you mind paying a small percent to have others market your product? How would it feel to have lots of people out there creating happy customers for you? This brings income to the creators (or owners) and the direct sellers. Here's how it works:

The money. A direct seller and network marketer introduces someone else directly to something of value, created by a third party. And if a sale is made, the direct seller gets a piece of the selling price. Call it a commission; an override; a percent; a piece of the action, etc. They get a piece of the price of the thing they sell INSTEAD of any regular salary. The piece they get averages from 3%-50% of the selling price. For personal retail sales, it can be 30%-50% of the selling price. For sales of others in their group, it ranges from 3%-10%.

Direct sellers are creators of something very valuable to the mother company: Loyal customers. ☺

People who earn their living through commissions off their direct sales are more common than many people think.

Have you bought or sold a home?

In real estate sales, an agent might call a prospective buyer to alert them about a property being available. This would have been unknown but for the focused work and quick call from the agent. The agent hopes she's the first to introduce the buyer to the property, so that if he's interested, the sale will be hers and a commission earned. It's a direct sale.

Movie scripts/book manuscripts

A literary agent might call a movie producer or publisher about a script that might be right for them. She hopes to be the first to introduce that script for the same reason. If it's sold, the agent gets a percent of the sales price, or of the advance the author gets.   Another direct sale.

Stocks and Securities

When a stock broker recommends an investment and a buyer goes for it, the broker gets a cut. That's a direct sale.

Vacuums, pots and pans, brushes, etc.

Have you ever opened the door to a vacuum cleaner salesman dying to show you how his machine will clean your carpets like never before? Or one who offers to cook you a feast on the latest kitchenware she's marketing for her company?

If you try it, love it and buy it, those sales people get paid a percent of the sales they make.

You get the idea.

While this kind of sales certainly earns money for the person who's selling, there's a small problem inherent in the situation. You know it, right?

They have to keep selling, selling, selling. Why?
Because. No sales = No money.

This is where regular direct sales companies and
the direct sales and network marketing industry
part ways.

There's a 'Hollywood edge' in most direct sales
done by network marketers.

7.
The Hollywood Edge of
Network Marketing Companies

With plain 100% commissioned sales positions, there is one giant drawback:

No sales = No money.

The real estate agent, the literary agent, and other direct sales people continually have to find more product to sell, i.e. a home, a script; or if they already have product, more right customers to introduce their product to. They need to close the deal or else. No sales means no money.

The 'no sales = no money' syndrome often makes people put big pressure on their prospects and customers. It can get so bad that customers run away, don't open their doors, and don't answer their phones if they suspect it's the seller calling. No one likes it when a person won't stop talking about his or her wares.

Here's the worst part: a regular direct sales person can never retire.

Network marketing companies have a way to overcome this problem. They have leverage.

The Hollywood edge

1. When a Direct Seller introduces someone to a product or service, and that product or service is one the customer wants to use on a regular basis rather than what they currently use, i.e. cable, phone, household products, nutritional or personal or pet care items, the direct seller earns a commission each time the product or service is reordered.

These are sales that the direct seller makes only once, at the time of the original sale. Each time the customer reorders, or when a product is shipped by the company on an automatic reorder plan, the Direct Seller who made the initial sale gets a percent of all that repeat business. Fun, huh?

Income from such repeat sales is referred to as 'residual income'.

2. In Hollywood, when an artist or producer of a song, a commercial, a movie or TV show has that 'repeat percent' in their contract, which the experienced ones do, they earn a commission each time their song or show airs. This income is also called 'residuals'. It's Hollywood at its best.

The dictionary definition of this repeat sale income or residual income is actually tied to Hollywood's practices.

Residual *n.*
A payment that is made to a performer or writer or director of a television show or commercial that is paid for every repeat showing: "he could retire on his residuals".[30]

---

[30] Source: *WordNet ® 1.6, © 1997 Princeton University*

That's leverage at work. Do work well once, and continue to get paid for it long after the work is done.

It's not just writers, producers, performers and direct sales people marketing products with the Hollywood edge that benefit from this kind of leverage.

Look at how a real estate developer makes his money. He builds an apartment complex, then rents it out and collects rent every month for years and years after the initial work is done.

Many people do not know how leverage works. No one ever showed them. So they scoff. Folks with closed minds don't realize the potential that this kind of leverage has to change lives.

For those in the know, this is precisely how they keep right on earning income, long AFTER they've made that initial direct sale, or done that initial 'work'. Network marketing and direct sales participants get paid for every repeat sale for years after they've made that original sale the first time. For those kinds of products that people pay for on a regular basis, of course,

That's the Hollywood edge.

This is one of the juiciest advantages that the network marketing industry has over other types of direct sales situations and traditional career options. Products people use and pay for on a regular basis are the kinds of products and services network marketing companies sell.

And for products network marketing companies market that are not 'consumable', there is yet another kind of leverage. It's the kind that comes from earning on the sales of other entrepreneurs. This will be described in other sections of this book.

By the way, did you know you give others residual income also? You do if you pay anything on a monthly basis - your mortgage, cable, rent, insurance, even your health club payments. These companies all get a little extra for themselves each time that payment comes in, yet they set up your cable only once, gave you a mortgage only once, showed you the workout club once or twice, and signed you up. See how that works?

If you want a smart Plan B, this is a good way to go.

How do people do this kind of Plan B?

Stories from 5 independent representatives

"Six years ago, I decided to become a direct seller of a new long distance service. I tried the service myself and my phone still worked, so that was all I needed to know. But to make money, I had to find my company a few customers to use the new long-distance service.

I asked my friends and family to help me get my business off the ground and to try it for a few months. Even though I 'm very lo-tech, I knew the company had lots of support people with technical expertise so I didn't have to become an expert on phone service. Knowing they'd back me up, I could tell everyone I'd be their personal telecom expert and mean it.

In the end, probably half said no and half said yes.

To say thanks, my husband and I baked dozens of yummy chocolate chip cookies, loaves of banana nut bread, even home baked pumpkin pies from pumpkins we grew.

Cookies were for the faraway customers; the pies and breads were for the folks within driving distance.

I didn't tell them they'd get cookies. That was a surprise reward for the ones who said yes.

My first customer related how she had received a check from AT&T a few months earlier for $50 to switch to them. She became their customer, then forgot about it. After she cashed the check, she had no loyalty to them.

Later, after she became my customer, she received our homemade pumpkin pie. She said she'd remember THAT for about 99 years. And so far, she has".[31] ☺

#2. Dave Johnson, in the top 1% of producers of publicly held NuSkin, relates:

"At a recent 10-year school reunion one of my former classmates asked me excitedly: 'Why is it that you don't look any older than when I saw you 10 years ago?' I told him, 'I have a secret about looking younger.' Of course, he was all ears and wanted to know just what it was that I was doing to keep my younger appearance.

It's at these kinds of opportunities that our business shines brightest. I sat down with him and shared the benefits of our NuSkin 180 Anti-Aging Skin Therapy System, which reduces the lines that occur at the derma layer of the skin. The result - Coni and I looking much younger than our driver's licenses reveal. It works so well for us, I've become addicted to this unique skin care system.

---

[31] Jacqueline Freeman is in the top 1% of the reps in Excel Communications, an alternative telecommunications networking company. thefreemans@myexcel.com

Even more amazing is that my friend purchased the 180 System and is still using it today. I mentioned that I could arrange to have it delivered automatically every month, one less thing for him to remember. Our automatic delivery program does that for us and the company sends me a residual commission on his and thousands of other customers who order regularly, every month.[32]

#3. Donna Johnson, the very top earner for Arbonne, tells us:

"The month I joined Arbonne, 15 years ago, I sat next to a nice lady on the plane from Chicago. I showed her my catalog, shared my excitement for the European natural skin care products, gave her my company's ID#, my 800#, and showed her how to order. A few days later she placed an order. 15 years later, she's still with me. I send her thank you cards, holiday cards, and other niceties. And, I have residual income. Not only from her, but

---

[32] Dave Johnson of NuSkin, Hawaiian Blue Diamond, Team Elite *carda@bigplanet.com*

thousands of others who use the products each month."

Of course, after 15 years with Arbonne, Donna now has thousands of people making those direct sales, and entrepreneurs doing the same thing. She receives a small percent on the efforts of thousands of people in her company, which is as it should be since without her, they would not be there helping Arbonne grow.[33]

Can you see the Hollywood edge in these examples?

#4. Jan Ruhe, a 23-year veteran in the network marketing industry, is the top earner for Discovery Toys. She has thousands of people in her organization. According to Jan,

"The Discovery Toy line is for parents who want their children to have an edge in the classroom, who want their children to

---

[33] **Error! Bookmark not defined.** the very top earner at Arbonne.

*have better vocabularies, communication skills,
leadership skills, and who really want their children
to have the best educational table top games and
software to grow up with. We introduce the
products to parents so they and their children can
experience them. Then they can decide."*

Jan has tens of thousands of people in her
organization who do direct sales of these
educational toys, and who find both customers and
entrepreneurial parents. In her case the products
themselves are not 'residual' in that a parent buys
them once, not each month. However, her leverage
comes from getting paid a small percent by her
grateful company on the direct sales toys by
thousands of people whom she did not personally
recruit into the business, or sign up as customers.
They all contribute to her income.[34]

#5. Dr. Roger Boger, a top banana at Nikken, has
built up an organization of tens of thousands over
the last 10 years as an independent rep for them.

---

[34] Jan Ruhe, Top Diamond Sales Director in annual earnings
year after year after year at Discovery Toys,

Like Discovery Toys, Nikken's reps also direct sell products, some which are not on a monthly renewal plan, and some which are. However, because the primary product line has helped so many thousands of people get rid of the little (and big) annoyances like those nagging backaches, or trouble sleeping, thousands of people, including Roger, have personally introduced hundreds of customers to the company's advanced sleep system.

Today, after 10 years, Dr. Boger has tens of thousands of customers and hundreds of entrepreneurs who are making introductions and offering experiences with these products, to anyone who'd like an alternative fix to some of these irritating problems. And he earns a percent on most all of their sales. That's leverage at work.[35]

---

[35] Dr. Roger Boger, Royal Diamond at Nikken,

The last two examples are Hollywood edge not because the products are Hollywood edge, but because the process of people earning on the efforts of others gives them that residual income also. Income for which they have done the work originally, and which keeps coming after they have done it.

How do companies find people like this who want to help them expand?

Two of the biggest secrets are strategies used by two household names.

64

8.
How They Get Top Producers Without Paying Salaries or Bonuses

Most people don't know that some big name companies get their top producers without paying upfront salaries or bonuses. Sometimes, people pay **them** instead.

It's a page right from the network marketing model.

1. McDonald's

To explain the success of McDonald's, in his uplifting and informative book, *McDonald's: Behind the Arches*, John Love says it was not the salaries (ha-ha) that attracted the good people they got to open and operate the stores, nor was it because the founder was famous or was a products or advertising genius. Love writes this instead about the legendary founder, Ray Kroc:

"Few people realized his true brilliance – **his ability to motivate and harness the power of hundreds of entrepreneurs. By enforcing rigid standards of quality, service and cleanliness among his franchisees** and suppliers, Kroc revolutionized the food service industry in the U.S. But by also **giving his franchisees enormous freedom in marketing,** he kept McDonald's fresh – and at the same time, created a franchising model that scores of other chains now emulate."[36]

Hmm. The marketing and expansion strategy Kroc used was to find, motivate and harness the power of hundreds of entrepreneurs. People who, despite being entrepreneurs, were held to a rigid quality and service standard, but who were still given marketing freedom. And most of them love that combination so much that they pay McDonald's VERY GOOD money for the privilege of helping it expand, and helping themselves as well.

---

[36] Love, John F. (1986), book jacket

Remember, these franchising entrepreneurs get no regular salary. And they often pay hundreds of thousands of dollars for a franchise. (!)

Here might be a hypothetical ad describing this kind of person:

Wanted: An entrepreneur who seeks a name and a system. who
1. wants to help market an established product line, AND
2. run their own show. AND
3. someone who can scrape up some major bucks.

(At McDonald's, qualified prospective franchisees receive a fat prospectus describing the investments and commitments the franchisee has to make.)

Business people know the entrepreneurs not only pay up front for a franchise (upwards of $1 million for a McDonald's franchise today), they pay a percent of their gross sales to the company besides. Ranges from 5-8%.[37]

Why would people pay so much for what some scoffing detractors call 'buying a job'?

Because some entrepreneurs want a sure-fire, recognizable name and product line to put their sweat behind. But, they still want to run their own store. The formula works fabulously well.

2. Amazon.com

Amazon's major expansion and meteoric rise in the late 1990's was due to their brilliant online associate (formerly called 'affiliate') program. Is there anyone who has ever been online who has not seen one of their cute and clever banners?

Did you know that Amazon's primary sales force, their associates, are all 100% commission sales help?

---

[37] ibid, p.152

According to the Amazon website, as of April 15, 2002, Amazon has "thousands of current Web sites participating in the Amazon.com Associates Program. We have over 500,000 Associates of all sizes and virtually every area of interest."[38]

Amazon's associates are responsible for a humongous percent of Amazon's sales, yet Amazon pays no money to its associates until they bring in a sale. The associate then gets a small percentage of the sale, 3%-10% or so, depending on the item.

Are you an associate? Then you know you get a percent of the sale each time your site rings up a purchase at Amazon.com.

Thousands of companies have similar affiliate and associate programs, altogether generating millions of dollars of online sales for those companies. And it's all accomplished by people who introduce others to the company's products and services, at no direct cost to the company until a sale is made.

38

http://www.amazon.com/exec/obidos/subst/associates/join/associates.html/103-7394794-2216632

All the parties seem to love it. 500,000 associates for Amazon online says it all.[39]

Here's a hypothetical ad describing what Amazon looks for in the way of sales help:

Wanted. Entrepreneur with website. Would you like to post a banner of the 'earth's largest online bookstore' on your site and earn a commission EACH time someone clicks on that banner and buys anything from us? No hassles. We drop-ship all orders for you. We even provide cool banners to attract more customers to your link to us.

Amazon is arguably the biggest force behind the affiliate marketing strategy online. Their banners are virtually everywhere.

Here's where these strategies of McDonald's and Amazon are a page from network marketing.

---

[39] Our own http://www.mlm911.com website for network marketers, which shows entrepreneurs how to build their own giant heap, also has a large affiliate program.

9.

Network Marketing Lets Individuals Do It

"I'd rather earn 3% off the efforts of 100 others than earn 100% of my own effort."[40]

Why should companies like McDonald's and Amazon be the only ones able to recruit entrepreneurs to help them market?

What if entrepreneurs could recruit other entrepreneurs to work with them?

They can. That's the concept behind network marketing.

You know network marketing companies make direct sales a big part of what their entrepreneurs do.

---

[40] Attributed at various times to John Paul Getty and John D. Rockefeller.

In addition, the network marketing entrepreneur can also introduce the **idea** of becoming a direct seller to another entrepreneur.

Here's how it works.

Say a network marketing company is introducing an advanced, natural, non-toxic anti-aging product that has been clinically proven to work. Or perhaps it is offering an alternative telecom or local phone service, with superb quality personal service attached. Or with an internet connection attached for the same price.

We all know that these new products and services are best introduced, experienced, or explained to a customer, like anything else that's either novel or an alternative to the status quo.

The entrepreneur and company agree that the entrepreneurs get paid whenever they make sales, and they can receive those Hollywood-edge repeat commissions every month after that.

And here's what separates a plain direct sales company from a network marketing one:

In a network marketing company the entrepreneur helps the company expand by finding other entrepreneurs to become direct sellers. Then, E #1 can earn a percent of the sales E #2 generates.

Isn't that the fair thing to do? Why should a company be the only one who gets paid for finding entrepreneurs?

Welcome to the primo Plan B: network marketing.

Direct sales and network marketing are ways to introduce new and alternative products and services directly to people who would otherwise never know about them. The products are not typically in stores nor advertised in mainstream ways. They're new, or are an alternative to the mainstream variety, and the customers need someone to show them how (and sometimes why) the product works.

Think how Estée Lauder and Michael Dell did that. They both did direct sales, which is a significant part of network marketing.

A network marketing entrepreneur does two things:

1. Direct sales. Introduces new and unique products and services directly to others who might want them, and builds a customer base to get that Hollywood-edge residual income.

2. Builds a Heap. Finds other entrepreneurs who want to do direct sales with the product or service they represent, build their own customer base, and perhaps find other entrepreneurs to do the same. From the sales of this network of people (= heap), receive more Hollywood-edge residual income.

But there's more.

Most network marketing companies pay on more than one level of customers and entrepreneurs in someone's heap. That's where the name 'multi-level' has its origin. It refers to HOW the company pays people for helping it introduce its products and services to the world.

The network marketing pay plan gives good entrepreneurial people and happy customers a reason to help spread the word about new products and services that the world might otherwise never hear about.

Smart, huh?

Each individual entrepreneur receives a small percent of the sales of many people in the heap for those she was responsible for bringing in directly or indirectly.

Even though the percents are small, this money can and does become substantial as the heap gets bigger. Especially the residual part.

An entrepreneur who chooses network marketing as their Plan B can build a little heap or a giant heap - a heap of both long-term customers and of entrepreneurs, who introduce still other customers and entrepreneurs to their new or alternative products and services.

If it's done right, a smart entrepreneur can earn an ongoing commission, month after month. Neat, huh?

Have I sold you? OK. Here's the catch:

It isn't easy.

As in any industry, network marketing has people who are in it for a quick buck. They gain by misrepresenting to others what it takes to be successful, and they cause emotional distress and financial losses to people they lured in by telling them that the business would be a cake walk. To say nothing of leaving a very bad taste in the mouths of those who were told it would be easy.

The network marketing business is not easy. There are reasons people become successful in this business as in any other, and you may as well learn now if you have what it takes or not.

10.
Who Should Consider
Network Marketing and Direct Sales
As Their Plan B?

On the book's cover, we announce that network marketing and direct sales, is

For Entrepreneurs only

en•tre•pre•neur n.   A person who organizes, operates, and assumes the risk for a business venture.[41]

What are the entrepreneurial risks a network marketer assumes?

1. There is no regular paycheck.
This comes as a shock to people who have never experienced doing anything on their own before. Someone who's been a mainstreamer all of their

---

[41] *The American Heritage® Dictionary of the English Language, Fourth Edition (2000), www.dictionary.com.*

adult life may have never really considered that entrepreneurs risk a regular paycheck in order to have a chance at something with a much bigger, but not a guaranteed, return.

2. You must put out time and honest effort before you see results
The amount and type of effort depends on how fast someone wants to go. Some people decide to sleep less, like Mary Kay did, to create those extra hours. Others decide to trade in say, TV time so they can spend it on Plan B.

3. **You must put out money and other resources before you see results.**
This too, may be news to some mainstreamers.

How much money? That depends on how fast you want to go, and what kinds of things you'll do to find new customers. Will you do direct mail? Email campaigns? Some business-to-business mutual support? Visit related businesses? Or contact acquaintances by personal letter?

Some people spend a few hundred dollars a month and 20-25 hours a week, while others spend several thousand a month, and 5 hours a week. There are always others doing it already to learn from.

Many people do their Plan B part time, so they can hold things together with the income from their regular job. So here's a heads up:

> WARNING: With any entrepreneurial Plan B, including network marketing and direct sales, there are NO GUARANTEES. It may take some years before someone earns enough of the Hollywood income to quit their regular job. Plan on 3-5 years at least. And face it, some people aren't cut out to take on these entrepreneurial risks and are better off going back to a mainstream job.

So what else does it take?

It takes brains, attitude and a sense of humor

In a section entitled "NO BOZO's NEED APPLY", author James Citrin, in his new book, ZOOM, relates an interview with Tim Koogle, former Yahoo! CEO. It's Koogle who led Yahoo! from a handful of people to its giant heights. Koogle says Yahoo!'s success came from the kind of people they hired. The attributes they sought from day one are the same ones it takes to make it in network marketing.

"We hire on the basis of two things: intelligence and proactive behavior, which involves attitude and a 'can do' spirit. In general these two things are much more important to us than specific experience. We look for these two things because the space in which we compete is changing so fast that people need to be able to figure out for themselves what needs to be done. So we look for if they're smart and if they have the right attitude."[42]

Another colorful description of who is likely to make it in a fast entrepreneurial environment comes from the chairman and CEO of Akamai, a major Internet player that receives 700 résumés

---

[42] Citrin, James M. (2002), p. 123

per week, but "invites only a handful of candidates in for interviews."

What is Akamai looking for in a potential hire? Like Yahoo! this is a company run by entrepreneurs, who seek people like themselves to join them. The same kind of people it takes to make it in network marketing. Here's from George Conrades, the CEO of Akamai:

"We look for employees who just love to pack as much stuff as they can into one day...great employees are also people who have a tremendous ambition. They really want do something. They want to effect change. Great employees are people who combine that ambition with being very smart. And so we place a premium on intelligence. **It's not that we are looking for good grades. We want to know if they can think.** So ambition, smarts, and energy are the factors that we look for!"[43]

---

[43] ibid, p. 51

Say a problem comes up with something, as it always does. Do you melt down and go, oh, this doesn't work? OR do you think, well, maybe we can do X instead; or this or that for now, while they fix that. So let's do this other thing now.

Add to that attitude a sense of humor, and you're well on your way.

So far then, we know it takes entrepreneurs who
1. can think
2. have a proactive attitude
3. have a sense of humor

What about belief? How much do you need to believe in the thing you are doing to make a go of it? There are some interesting sides to this concept. First, those who say you must believe it to achieve it.

> "Luke: I don't believe it.
> Yoda: That is why you fail."[44]

---

[44] *Star Wars* (1980), Episode V: The Empire Strikes Back

At the other end, have you heard those who HAVE achieved, who say they never would have believed it, if they hadn't seen it?

> "If our neighbor, Tim, had told us at first that we'd be making the kind of money we are making now, we would not have believed him. We had people before him tell us we could make $1,000,000 a year, but we just laughed and sent them away. We both thought it was dishonest and just BS to make such claims, and we could never say such things to others. Not even now. We still find it hard to believe. Even now we have to pinch ourselves once in a while."[45]

Or consider what John D. Rockefeller wrote in his memoirs:

> "None of us ever dreamed of the magnitude of what proved to be the later expansion [of our business]. We did our day's work as we

---

[45] Bob and Sue Burdick, top bananas, making major gangster money, as NSA independent reps

met it, looking forward to what we could see in the distance and keeping well up to our opportunities, but laying our foundations firmly."[46]

As did Mary Kay Ash:

"Mary Kay Cosmetics turned out to surpass my wildest dreams. I never could have predicted that the company would grow to even a fraction of its present size or that it would do a fraction of the good it has done."[47]

So, how do these examples square with "You must believe to achieve?" Especially those who like to think big from the outset?

Perhaps Napoleon Hill best captures both ends of the belief phenomenon:

---

[46] John D. Rockefeller (1984), p. 8
[47] Mary Kay Ash (1995), p. 140

"Anything the mind can believe, it can achieve".[48]

It is the 'thing' in 'anything' that differs for people. How far out there, or close in, does that thing have to be to motivate you?

Are you someone who is energized by seeing the VERY end of a specific trip? Say you're driving from Los Angeles to New York. Do you keep your navigational system in your car set on how many miles to New York when you're still in Los Angeles or Phoenix? Or do you chunk it down into smaller milestones, and set your system to the next big city, like Phoenix, if you're starting in Los Angeles?

Keeping the end in mind is a wonderful and efficient way to get somewhere, including in a business. But people can choose in-between ends and far-out ends. Same is true with the added income a Plan B might provide.

Picturing an additional $200 more per month may be more doable for someone starting out than

---

[48] Napoleon Hill (1937/1988), p. 70.

trying to picture an additional say, $5000 more per month. Although someone else might prefer to picture the bigger number from the get-go.

The believability factor is different for different people. Thinking big in small steps works for lots of people.

"Take the first step in faith. You don't have to see the whole staircase, just take the first step." Dr. Martin Luther King Jr.

Others are more inspired by keeping the top of the staircase in their minds.

Perhaps what matters most here is belief in the process of doing and practicing the things that work that others have done, and of trying new things.

Ponder this recent finding on the role of practice:

"There have now been many studies of elite performers-...and the biggest difference researchers find between them and lesser

performers is the amount of deliberate practice they've accumulated. Indeed, the most important talent may be the talent for practice itself..."[49]

Belief in practice, in being proactive, and not freezing or giving up if you don't know for sure if one or the other thing you'll do is going to work or not. Much like driving in the fog. You can't see ahead too well, but you're moving forward anyway.

So what if you take a wrong turn? Who hasn't? Successful entrepreneurs go back and try another route. And reframe it to boot.

"We are not retreating - we are advancing in another direction.
-General Douglas MacArthur" (1880-1964)

Emerson said it best: "Do the thing; get the power".[50] Where do=over and over.

---

[49] A. Gawande in "Annals of Medicine' The Learning Curve'" New Yorker magazine, 2.02
[50] Ralph Waldo Emerson (1982) p.181

Does the thought of taking action alone cause you to freeze? Many people find buddy and do things together. Just like working out or doing anything that is easier not to do. What if the belief comes after you see and experience what you achieve together?

In summary, here's who should consider network marketing. Entrepreneurs who

1. can think
2. have a proactive attitude
3. have a sense of humor
4. believe in the process of doing and practicing the things it takes to advance.

Now comes the final hurdle.

11.
Can You Take the Heat?
Part I. The Pukies.

Network marketers and direct sellers take some big heat. If you want to make it, learn to take it.

The two great heat generators: pukies and pyramids.

Pukies[51] first.

puke·y <u>Pronunciation Key</u> (pyo͞o′kē) *n.*

a.   Someone who ridicules, condemns, or belittles a new idea or thing

b.   Someone who has attempted to do network marketing or direct sales, has failed and now announces that no one else can do it either,

---

[51] This was first used by Kim Klaver in the early 1990s and first appeared in the audio tape, So, You want to be a Networker? Kim Klaver. 1996. Max Out Productions

because obviously it doesn't work, is no good, they're all crooks, etc. Opinion often accompanied by hysteria.

New ideas, new concepts, innovative ways of thinking and doing things seem to draw out the pukies within us. Yuck. Get out the pukey umbrella if you're venturing out to do something different, like network marketing or direct sales.

Pukies have plagued every person with new ideas throughout the ages. At least, when you try something new, you'll be in good company. Here are a few others whose names may be familiar, who have had to bear pukies before you.

Jesus – He had some new ideas, definitely not consistent with the mainstream authorities of the day. Look what they did to him.

Copernicus - Did you know the great astronomer and mathematician got puked on, publicly, by his contemporary, Martin Luther, for his revolutionary ideas? Even though Martin Luther was himself a kind of revolutionary (he broke from the traditional Catholic Church to start his own denomination, the Lutherans).

Still, Martin was a pukey when it came to things he didn't know about firsthand, that went against his beliefs and knowledge. He went hysterical about the work of Copernicus...

"People give ear to an upstart astrologer who strove to show that the earth revolves, not the heavens, the sun and the moon...This fool wishes to reverse the entire science of astronomy..." Martin Luther, 1533, speaking of Copernicus[52]

Copernicus was distraught by his attackers, too, but he continued on despite them.

"...the scorn which I had to fear on account of the newness and absurdity of my opinion almost drove me to abandon a work already undertaken."[53]

---

[52] Kim Klaver (1998), p. 21
[53] Ibid, p. 22

Galileo - He was publicly humiliated and accused of heresy by the Church in the early 1600s, a very big deal, and was forced to publicly state that he "cursed and detested his errors and heresies contrary to the Holy Church".

In the documents found, he was tried and sentenced to prison by the Church for suggesting that the sun, instead of the earth, might be the center of the universe.[54]

Of course, Galileo, then 70, did as he was sentenced, since the excommunication from the church meant, to him as it did to other Catholics of that time, that he could not enter heaven. So he disavowed his entire life's work that day in 1633. But, he had his telescope and knew what he had seen up in the skies.

Not one of the three Cardinals at his inquisition had any scientific training, and none had ever looked through a telescope.

---

[54] Ibid, p. 23, for the entire text of Galileo's sentence and his denouncement of his own work.

Columbus – Did you know he petitioned the governments of Portugal, France and Spain for seven years before Spain's Queen Isabella finally backed him for his crazy trip to the Americas? Want to know what his contemporaries said about him?

"Because of his impatience with all who were slow to be convinced, Columbus was considered a little touched in the head...a fool to some and a bore to most...and the worst of it was, he had to persuade stupid people in high places that his enterprise was plausible...because he wanted money, men and equipment."[55]

Lord Kelvin – This gent was president of England's Royal Society from 1890-1895 and he publicly declared to all: "Radios have no future; X-Rays are a hoax; Flying machines are impossible." Think that might be one reason an Italian invented radio? Because the English inventors were discouraged

---

[55] Samuel Eliot Morison (1983), p. 84

and gave up when they heard the big wig's negative pronouncements?[56]

Edison – In 1879, Edison announced his intent to light up a city block within months, for all to witness. The scientific establishment and newspapers wrote sneery headlines to the world about Edison and his plans like "What a self promoting humbug" and "Sheer nonsense."[57]

On New Year's Eve 6 months later, in Menlo Park, New Jersey, Edison stunned and delighted hundreds of writers and thousands of bystanders when he lit up an entire city block with over 100 light bulbs.[58]

And did you know what happened to the "patron saint of invention itself"[59], with 1000+ patents to his name, including patents for inventing the

---

[56] Mary Kay Ash (1995), pp. 88-89

[57] Kim Klaver (1998), p. 25

[58] ibid p. 25

[59] John Schwartz, April 4, 2002, *The New York Times.* "Living on Internet Time in Another Age". p. E1.

incandescent light bulb, the phonograph, electricity, and moving pictures, when he was a child?

When Thomas was second grade, he didn't respond the way the mainstream teachers expected. You know, about mainstream things that were expected of mainstream second graders.

Teachers then and now have been trained to prepare the youngsters for a traditional mainstream life and job. But little Thomas was not destined to be one of them.

One day, when this little guy was just in the second grade, the school sent him home early with a note to his parents, which read:

"Your son, Thomas Edison, has an addled mind and cannot take an education."[60]

They asked him not to come back to school, and he never went another day. Fortunately for the

---

[60] Napoleon Hill (1993), Audio tapes

world, he turned out, anyway. He got those pukies early on.

President John Adams - The pukies our second president got were political adversaries. And they said hair-raising things. One of his detractors, a propagandist named James Callender, did not want "the wretch" Adams elected President. He called Adams, when he was President, in his writings

"A 'repulsive pedant' and 'gross hypocrite' and 'in his private life, one of the most egregious fools upon the continent.' Adams was 'that strange compound of ignorance and ferocity, of deceit and weakness,' a 'hideous hermaphroditical character which has neither the force and firmness of a man, nor the gentleness and sensibility of a woman.'"[61]

Of course Adams was furious. Over many years, however, President Adams learned pukies come to anyone who creates change. Adams' autobiographer relates this change in his attitude, which came late is his life:

---

[61] David McCullough (2001), p. 537

"Adverse comments about his own role in public life that appeared occasionally in print, or the 'strange' letters he occasionally received, were no longer of any matter to him. They were like insects buzzing about, he told [his son] John Quincy. 'Their bite in former times tingled, but I am grown almost as insensible as a Boston dray horse in September.'"[62]

Pukey family and friends –They're the worst, because they know you and don't spare words or attitude. Even though they may be entirely wrong.

Family and friends have done more to deflate the egos and futures of budding entrepreneurs than anyone else in the history of mankind. VERY strange, in my opinion. Why wouldn't one support someone they say they love, who's trying to break out of the mold? The mold isn't that great, is it?

If you're a family member or friend of an entrepreneur, why not be supportive and help them at least try to get out of the mainstream if they

---

[62] ibid, p. 615

want to? After all, what if their thing DOES work? No one appears to be exempt.

John D. Rockefeller - The founder of the great Standard Oil Company, wrote:

"I well remember my old and distinguished friend, Rev. Thomas W. Armitage, for some forty years pastor of a great New York church, warning me that it was worse than folly to extend our plants and our operations. He was sure we were running unwarranted risks, that our oil supply would probably fail, the demand would decline, and he, with many others, sometimes I thought almost everybody, prophesied ruin."[63]

Mary Kay Ash – The founder of Mary Kay Cosmetics, a direct sales company with over 400,000 independent representatives, wrote in her autobiography:

---

[63] John D. Rockefeller (1984), p. 8

"...friends and relatives (may) forecast your ruin. In my case, my accountant and lawyer both warned me, 'for my own good' to abort my plans to go into business. They pleaded, 'Mary Kay, don't throw away your life's savings (of $5k). You know nothing about the cosmetics business'...they even sent me a pamphlet from Washington D.C. stating how many cosmetics companies went out of business everyday. Had I listened to their advice, MKC would have never opened its doors."[64]

Michael Dell - Like Estée Lauder's father, Michael Dell's parents didn't want their son, in college at the time he got caught up in creating his business, to neglect his academic work for any business.

"Michael's parents grew increasingly worried that he was neglecting his academic work for business interests. In the fall, Alexander and Lorraine Dell flew to Austin for a surprise visit, calling Michael from the airport. He barely had time to hide the computers in his roommate's shower before they

---

[64] Mary Kay Ash (1995), p. 87

arrived. Arguments erupted between parents and son. But, like Esty Lauder, he couldn't stop.

"Despite his parents' objections, Michael could not resist the opportunity he saw before him. He moved his operation out of his dorm room and into a two-bedroom condominium."[65]

Top people in network marketing companies have also had to endure pukies, scorn and ridicule before, during and even AFTER they've become wildly successful. Here are experiences of a few I know personally.

Paula Pritchard - 25-year network marketing vet, who climbed to the top of five major networking companies (Amway, Herbalife, NSA, Quorum, I-Link and starting again with Viogenix and Telewrx):

"For the first eight years of my network marketing career, I couldn't even say my company's name. People's perceptions of network marketing and the company I represented then – Amway – was so bad.

---

[65] Nancy Koehn (2001), p. 287

They'd say, 'you're gonna give up teaching at the university to sell soap?' When I was there, we all survived by listening to tape after tape of people's horror stories about the pukies and how they kept on despite them. Those years make me what I am...puke-proof, as Kim would say."[66]

Usa Johnson – Usa is in the top 1% of earners at Morinda. She says, "I myself was very cautious the first time I was introduced to network marketing. Never in 2 million years did I think I'd be doing something like this. I have had many friends look at me funny when I approached them with my opportunity. Now it is easier because I succeeded despite what they said."[67]

Ray Gebauer – Ray, top banana in Mannatech, says "I've had pukey family and friends my entire 27 years of networking, and even now, when I'm the most successful person they know, most of them still are, you know, pukey."[68]

---

[66] Paulais@hotmail.com

[67] cnn@comcast.net

[68] starmakr@nwlink.com

Finally, weighing in on the effect of friends and family is Napoleon Hill, author of the much-cited work, *Think and Grow Rich*. He spent 20 years of intensive, full time research on what makes someone successful. He conducted hundreds of interviews in the kitchens of Andrew Carnegie, Henry Ford, Thomas Edison, John D Rockefeller, and concluded this about friends and family:

"Close friends and relatives...often handicap one through 'opinions' and ridicule...thousands of men and women carry inferiority complexes with them all through life, because some well-meaning but ignorant person destroyed their confidence through 'opinions' or ridicule."[69]

Here are three suggestions to avoid catching pukey fever that people have used with success. Pukey fever refers to those inner voices telling you that maybe you really can't do it after all.

---

[69] Napoleon Hill (1990), p. 140-141

1. **"No be there. Duck"** In the movie, Karate Kid, that's what the Karate trainer, Mr. Miyagi said to the Karate kid-in-training when the lad asked what he should do next time the bigger boys, with black belts, would kick or punch him.

Do you agree?

Two ways to duck those pukies in network marketing and direct sales:

a) Learn reaching out methods to draw out the right people for your product, so they come to you instead of you going to them (e.g. do focused ads, direct mail, email campaigns[70] etc.),

b) Learn to say no first to the wrong ones.[71]

---

[70] Kim Klaver (1998) pp. 85-148
[71] Kim Klaver (1998), pp. 29-39

2. **Consider the source.** Two things to help you here.

   a) Ask the person, after they say their pukey thing: **"How do you know this?"** Wait for the reply. Then decide how much weight, if any, to give it.

   If you want to make it in acting, whom would you listen to? Tom Cruise or Julia Roberts? Or to someone who hasn't made it and who's telling you what's wrong with the acting industry?

   b) Ask yourself: Do I want to be like this person? Financially, health-wise, attitude-wise?

3. **Decide what kinds of people you want to associate with for your business.**
   Do you want to associate with people who bring out the worst in you? Doubts, fears and hesitations? Or who bring out the best in you? Proactive people who are willing to step outside the mainstream to make a go of

it, people who keep innovating and moving ahead with you?

Stick with like-minded people to do your business, and do things in teams, so you can lend each other your skills and mental attitudes.

So there you have it about the pukies. Get ready. They will come. They always have. ☹

12.
Can You Take the Heat?
Part II. Those Pyramids.

Chances are good that if you take on network marketing and direct sales as your Plan B, you'll be asked everyone's favorite question (ha-ha):

Is this a pyramid? ☹

What they may really be asking is:

Is this a pyramid *scheme?*

Here's the definition of a pyramid scheme, according to American Heritage dictionary:

pyr·a·mid scheme *n.*

A fraudulent money-making scheme in which people are recruited to make payments to others above them in a hierarchy while expecting to receive payments from people recruited below them. Eventually the number of new recruits fails to sustain the payment structure, and the scheme collapses with most people losing the money they paid in.[72]

Here's an expanded description.

"Pyramid schemes focus on the exchange of money and recruitment. At the heart of each pyramid scheme there is typically a representation that new participants can recoup their original investments by inducing two or more prospects to make the same investment.

For each person you bring in you are promised future monetary rewards or bonuses based on your advancement up the structure. Over time, the hierarchy of participants resembles a pyramid as newer, larger layers of participants join the established structure at the bottom.
They say you will have to do "little or no work because the people below you will". You should be aware that the actual business of sales and

---

[72] The American Heritage Dictionary of the English Language, Fourth Edition (2000), www.dictionary.com.

supervision is hard work. So if everyone is doing little or no work, how successful can a venture be?

The marketing of a product or service, if done at all, is only of secondary importance in an attempt to evade prosecution or to provide a corporate substance. Often there is not even an established market for the products so the "sale" of such merchandise, newsletters or services is used as a front for transactions which occur only among and between the operation's distributors.

Therefore, your earning potential depends primarily on how many people you sign up, not how much merchandise is sold. "[73]

A big clue that you're dealing with a pyramid scheme with nothing real to bring to market is the make-big-money and requires-little-or-no-work pitch.

---

[73] http://www.crimes-of-persuasion.com/Crimes/ Delivered/pyramids.htm

People making these pitches are either hopelessly ignorant or are not selling anything tangible.

They're selling you the opportunity to sell the scheme to someone else, and hope you'll buy in so that they're not left holding the bag themselves.

If you're not sure about an offer you're interested in, ask. For example:

"What do you market and can I see it, try it or experience it?" Then you try it and evaluate it. If you get nothing, or nothing you feel is valuable, keep moving. Far, far away.

While it may be tempting sometimes to go for something that looks like a quick return, I side with the great John D. Rockefeller, who saw lots of quick buck artists in his day as well:

"Sometimes I feel that we Americans think we can find a short road to success, and it may appear that often this fact is accomplished; but real efficiency in work comes from knowing your facts and building up that sure foundation."[74]

The majority of network marketing and direct sales companies are not only legit, but have real alternatives to mainstream products and services. This is why in 2000 over 11 million people were involved in it, according to the Direct Selling Association.[75]

One reason companies choose network marketing to introduce the world to their products and services is because most don't start out with the giant coffers of big companies like General Motors, Microsoft or Proctor and Gamble. They use the network marketing model and word of mouth to introduce their goods into the market. And it works when companies have products and services people want. Amway does $5 billion a year with that model. Mary Kay does $2 billion. Both are now public companies. There are hundreds of others.

---

[74] John D. Rockefeller, (1984), Book Jacket
[75] http://www.dsa.org/research/numbers.htm#PEOPLE

Regarding the pyramid structure, all human organizations are pyramids. Think of the Catholic Church, for example. How many Popes at the top? They have their 'front line' the Cardinals, who have under them the Archbishops, etc. and the millions of parishioners are at the bottom.

Our government is the same. There's one President, with his front line cabinet members, each of whom have their people underneath them, etc. Corporations are the same - one CEO or president, then the lieutenants, all the way down - in their order of responsibility. Workers are at the bottom, with their little heaps and fiefdoms as well.

So if you ask someone the pyramid question about her business, be specific about the 'scheme' part of it. Since all human organizations are in a pyramid shape, but are not pyramid schemes.

And if someone asks you, if you are or become a network marketer, if your business is a pyramid scheme or even just a pyramid, describe what you do to make this clear. For example:

THEM: Is this a pyramid scheme?

YOU: Well, let me tell you what we do and you can call it whatever you want, OK?

THEM: OK.

YOU: We introduce and market products and services directly to consumers, people like you and me, and we find entrepreneurs who want to do it with us. The company pays us to do that because that's how they expand. Think you could do something like that if we showed you what to do? Or would you like to try the product/service and see if it works for you the way it has for me?

This way, you've stated the facts, without hype, and the listener can make their decision based on that, not some misconception about schemes involving people who are just taking money from each other hoping they won't be the last one left.

Network marketing and direct sales companies are a brilliant and cost effective way of directly introducing people to new, innovative or alternative products or services that they would otherwise never hear about.

If you are considering network marketing seriously, here are some things you should know. Tips from those who have gone before you.

13.
"Things I Wish Someone Had Told Me before I Got Involved in the Network Marketing Business."

It is true you are an independent contractor when you do network marketing. However, it is also true that if you have never done network marketing, or have never done it successfully, that the way it was presented to you may well be the way you present it to others. You want to be sure you didn't pick up any uh, scam quality pitch lines.

Here is the list of things most often mentioned by people in the network marketing business right now that they say they wish they had known before they got started.

"Things I wish someone had told me before I got involved in the network marketing business."

1. *It's not as easy as they said it would be.*

2. *I didn't expect the reactions I got from people I knew. I was shocked and flabbergasted.*

3. *There's more to it than just talking to people you know. There are leads you can use instead.*

4. *The odds. I had no idea how few people have what it takes to be an entrepreneur. Complaining and doing something about it are very different, I've found out.*

5. *It takes a certain attitude to make it. Backbone. I didn't expect that.*

6. *It may take a while before you make a profit. The cost of doing the business was never mentioned.*

7.	*It may take longer than you think. I'm a go-getter and I thought it would be a slam dunk. But it wasn't. I got pukies! I'm still getting over it. They took away some of my self-confidence.*

8.	*No one showed me what to do in the business, except to make your list of 100 people and call them all. Not a good experience.*

9.	*You risk your reputation – referring people you know and telling them it's good and getting paid on it, too.*

10.	*They say it's not sales, but it is. Isn't it?*

11.	*It's NOT for everyone. Not the business, nor the products and service.*

12.	*It takes time away from doing other things with your family.*

13. *You're risking bruising your own emotions. And your self-esteem. It's scary to go out on your own and hear no.*

14. *What to do with a new recruit? I wasn't ready to show them what to do. Except for the list of 100, which I couldn't in good faith tell anyone I know to do, after my experience.*

And still, many of these same people admit they are telling their new people the same things...that 'all they have to do' is make their list of 100 friends, family and neighbors.

Why?

Because, they say, 'That's what they said works.'

Recently, one seasoned network marketer on my weekly national conference call even compared this age-old problem to children who are abused by their parents, and who swear they'll never do that to their children, *and then, they end up doing the same thing to their children, anyway. And they can't believe they're doing that!*[76]

This is not a good thing.

Some people might not have done the business at all if they had known what to expect. But maybe that would have been a good thing.

Why talk a person into something they really are not suited to do, either psychologically, financially, or time-wise, by telling them nonsense that they don't recognize as such, or outright lies?

Is it really a good strategy to build a business with the wrong people?

Whether someone focuses on finding steady customers for the product (and earns those Hollywood residuals on the continued monthly product or service sales), or whether one finds other entrepreneurs to do direct sales:

---

[76] http://www.mlm911.com/events.html Call of 5.17.02

> Network marketing as a Plan B is for
> entrepreneurs only.

Of course people have succeeded and continue to succeed. However, in building a customer base or finding the right entrepreneurs, there is some risk.

It is NOT easy and anyone can NOT do it. Despite what anyone tells you in front of the room. If it were so easy, and if anyone could do it, how come so many people don't make it?

Of course there are people in the industry who cannot or will not acknowledge the truth of what it takes to make it. Or they worry they might scare off potential recruits.

Still, despite what these folks say, most people are better off staying in the mainstream. Why? Because they demonstrate, just by their initial questions (e.g. Do I have to spend money?) that they may not yet be ready to accept the risks or put out the effort required to make any Plan B work.

That includes network marketing.

Mary Kay advises would be entrepreneurs:

"...choose something you will enjoy...because during the first few years of your venture, you'll be required to put in a great deal of overtime...if hard work and long hours aren't what you have in mind, don't start your own business."[77]

---

[77] Mary Kay Ash (1995), p. 140

14.
People to Stay Away from When Choosing a Business

You're on your own if you sign with anyone who says any of the following things to induce you to join with them.

☹ 1. "It's easy. Anyone can do it."

☹ 2. "You can make big money almost immediately in this business."

☹ 3. "Everyone will want this product/service"

☹ 4. "Ours (this) is the best [deal/company/pay plan/management (you name it)] out there."

☹ 5. All you have to do is talk to people you know.

Let's take a quick look at why each of these should throw up a red flag for you.

☹ 1. "It's easy. Anyone can do it."

While it may be true that a Harvard degree is not required to make it big in networking, if it's so easy and anyone can do it, why isn't everyone making it? 100% false.

☹ 2. "You can make big money almost immediately in this business."

Another crock. The majority do NOT make it at all, much less make big money. Besides, what is 'big' money anyway?

In ANY entrepreneurial venture, dotcoms, new music groups, new TV shows, movies, you name it - the majority do not make money. Although a definitive study has not been made, the SBA says most new business startups go under within the first three years.

Some people in Network marketing DO make unbelievable income. But it is not easy, nor is it immediate. It is most assuredly not guaranteed.

☹ **3. "'Everyone' will want this product/service"**

This is what almost every network marketing company says about its services and product lines. Actually, it's what most every company out there says about their wares. Isn't it?
However it is totally false. **'Everyone' will not want any particular product or service**.

That's why a skilled and savvy marketer takes some time and first determines who the people and businesses are that are more likely to be predisposed to their wares. Michael Dell did that. John D. Rockefeller did that. Think you'll learn how to do that from someone who says #3? (See Chapter 17 for tips.)

☹ **4. "Ours is the best [deal/company/pay plan/management (you name it)] out there."**

Isn't this a matter of opinion? Even when people try the same things, they come out with different preferences.

Depends on your taste.

#4 is what almost every company says about themselves. Would you expect them to say otherwise?

Is anyone really listening? Saying something different than #4 has wonderful consequences. Think Avis, whose slogan 'we try harder' because they're #2 has made them a household name. America has been in love with the underdog forever.

For tips on how to write ad and talk copy that describes your predisposed markets, see Chapter 17.[78]

☹ **5. All you have to do is talk to people you know.**

If you hear this, run. It isn't true for 99.9% of people out there who are trying to earn at least a part-time income from their network marketing

---

[78] Also   and
http://www.mlm911.com

business. More than an extra $200 per month, anyway

In what business is it the case that 'all one has to do' is ANYTHING? There's always lots to do to make a business run.

Going to friends and family today (unless they're seasoned networkers) with your network marketing business or products, has been the #1 reason people new to this business say they haven't made it.

Friends and family don't often see what you see, so they react in ways no one is ready for. New networkers report that they are nearly always shocked, stunned and hurt at the reactions of people they know. Slowly, they begin to lose whatever self-confidence they had. Because of course they think it must be them. After all, the people in front of the room said it was easy, didn't they?

The worst pukies are friends and family. And it doesn't take many of these reactions. Three to ten, usually, before the new recruit is out of the game ☹. (See Chapter 11, Can you take the heat?)

Remember what Mr. Napoleon Hill said about the deadly effect of friends and family on one's plans for a new career or new ideas in his wonderful book, *Think and Grow Rich:*

"Close friends and relatives...often handicap one through 'opinions' and...ridicule...meant to be humorous. Thousands of men and women carry inferiority complexes with them all through life, because some well-meaning but ignorant person destroyed their confidence through 'opinions' or ridicule."[79]

---

[79] Napoleon Hill (1990), pp. 140-141

15.
Mainstream vs. Grass Roots Marketing

Mainstream companies let the world know about the products and services they've created through the mainstream media and the middle people who help make that happen. The public sees what's available on TV, radio, in all the print media, on the Internet and the like. And of course mainstream companies' goods and services are on display in retail stores everywhere.

This approach takes major advertising dollars. Tens of millions of dollars per year for big mainstream companies. However, like everything else, results are not guaranteed. Superbowl TV spots last year cost $2 million+ for a 30 second spot. Some of those companies' ads did not get results. Goodbye $2 million. ☹

Network marketing companies also want to let the world know about their products and services.

However, networking companies either are or they partner up with manufacturers of new or alternative products or services.

Then, they go find their marketing partners.

And it's not any big money partners or expensive Madison Avenue advertising companies.

Network marketing companies partner up with a grass roots sales force of independent distributors. That sales force, comprised of hundreds and thousands of network marketers, often across the globe, both fuels and funds the marketing effort. In exchange, the marketers get more money for their work than if they were salaried sales people, because the companies aren't paying the big money for salaries, advertising companies, middle people or the media. Instead, each individual does her own marketing and the company pays for results only.

The companies pay their hundreds and thousands of grass roots marketing partners commissions based on the new customers they bring in and the new entrepreneurs they locate who also find new customers. In other words, the companies share their wealth with their many partners who invest their time, energy and money with them.

No single person needs to invest those millions, because the money and effort invested is spread over so many people.

Here's how individual marketers typically approach others.

Some introduce others to a product or service because they personally love it, or have been affected significantly by it. Many have experienced a real life change.

So while they earn a living in the business, these folks do not sell for the money, but for the satisfaction of offering change to others and seeing others benefit, especially people they know. 'Share' is closest to the feeling they have about what they do.

Others picture and describe how it might be if hundreds or thousands of people who are either predisposed to a product or service, or who are ready for an alternative career, were to jump on the band wagon. They envision the financial potential of thousands of new customers and entrepreneurs that could become part of the person's business, if these good prospects just knew about it. So they describe and sell the vision, the dream, if you will.

Both approaches work. Depends completely on the individual marketer's personality.

Here are the two marketing jobs of a network marketer:

> 1. Build a customer base through direct sales. Introduce and market novel or alternative products and services to others who might not have heard about them otherwise.
>
> 2. Build a network. Find and introduce other entrepreneurs to the opportunity to do the same thing.

The result of the first activity is a customer base, contributing that Hollywood residual income to the individual marketer. The second activity results in a base of entrepreneurs that become part of the person's network or organization, which we call their heap, and which also contributes to the residual income of the individual who brought them in.

That's how it works.

So now, what does it take to build a successful network marketing business?

16.
What Does it Take to Build a Successful Network Marketing Business?

That is a good first question to ask the person you're thinking of signing up with.

If you get a response that is some mix of things those people say that we recommend you stay away from then do that (see Chapter 14). Find a smarter, more knowledgeable sponsor.

To make sure that YOU are not going into network marketing and direct sales as an unknowing buyer here's a quick overview of what it takes to make it.

1. Be prepared
2. Accept your mission
3. Know your odds
4. Learn and practice 3-5 methods of reaching out
5. Say no first
6. Do it in teams
7. Plan your time and money budget

8. Smile. Lighten up. Make introductions, not speeches. Skip hype.

#1. Be prepared

People who succeed at network marketing are those that not only learn to do their own jobs, but who can **build a team** by **showing** others to do the same kinds of things (not telling them – showing them). That means first, get prepared.

According to Millard Fuller, Founder of Habitat for Humanity, the 25-yr old company that builds teams and brings volunteers together everyday around the world to build homes for low-income families,

"One of the two most essential ingredients to creating a successful team is preparation. Doing all the background work. That way the work goes smoothly because as soon as the volunteers arrive, they have something productive to do and someone there who is qualified to show them how to do it."[80] Learn the different methods of reaching out, for example, so you can show them to others.[81]

#2. Accept your mission.

> **Your Mission:** *Find people for whom the product or service, or the business, is the right thing to be doing now, no one else.*[82]

Henry Heinz had to find people who wanted his home made quality pickles, Rockefeller decided to seek out merchants who were connected in some way with his business, Estée Lauder had to find women who were likely to want her skin care products, and Dell went after people he thought might want to buy a computer along with some knowledgeable instruction on how to use it. They

---

[80] *Fast Company* Magazine, November 2000

[81] Kim Klaver (1998) p.18

[82] Kim Klaver (1996), Audio cassette
Kim Klaver (1998), p. 18
And on

each went directly to the customers in the beginning, not vice versa.

The customers at the time had never heard of any of these folks or their products and services, but they were already predisposed towards them. How? Because these entrepreneurs determined who those people were that might be already inclined to their wares. That's what saved them so much time that others waste.

"Finding the other interested party is the first problem in most markets..."[83]

And you want that in your lifetime, of course.

---

[83] Bill Gates (1999), p. 73

#3. Know your odds.

> **The bad news.** *On average, the number of people out there for whom any product or service is the 'right' thing, including the network marketing business, has been 1/2 of 1% to about 8%. Higher for the products and services, lower for the business.*[84]
> **The good news.** *It doesn't take very many to make a success of it.*

Finding those right people for your products or services or the business is like shopping for shoes. Except you're shopping for people.[85]

---

[84] Misery loves company it seems. In July, 2001, Rear Admiral Volker, the head of Navy Recruiting, gave out this startling information:
* Navy Recruiters speak with 80-100 contacts to generate ONE recruit.
* The cost of recruiting each new service member is $9000, and $12,000 for the Army.
* Navy Recruiters are now trained by top professional sales trainers.

[85] Kim Klaver (1996) Audiotape

Like shoes, most people are not the right fit for your particular wares. That's the painful part. Each person has to discover the one out of ten who IS a fit. And discover that they do, firsthand, going through all ten, one by one. The trick is to survive that in your face qualification process. You know how it is...like being turned down by the first nine people you ask to the Prom. Ouch.

On the other hand, you wouldn't want to be without choices yourself, would you? Think of the many brands of cars, bread, or toothpaste. You just choose one and leave all the rest. People like to shop around. Including for mates. Remember the line in the old song "My momma told me, you better shop around."[86]

Shopping around is good. When you're the one shopping, of course. However, we can ease the pain of it when you're on the other side of the shopping table. We'll show you how to find those who are predisposed to what you have in the first place in Chapter 17.

---

[86] The Miracles. 1960. *Shop Around.* Motown

Here's the good news about the odds. It doesn't take that many customers or other entrepreneurs who choose your products or services to make a success of the business.

While 'success' is subjective, let me give you an example and a statistic that may surprise you.

How many customers does it take?

Say you are marketing a product that people buy for $50 per month. A nutritional supplement, for example. If you earn $10 from each sale each month from your own customers, and if you had 100 customers, you'd be earning $1000 per month.

Granted, not a fortune, but nice if it comes in every month like those Hollywood residuals. Which is exactly what happens if you're marketing a product people buy on a monthly basis. Need more money each month? Introduce the product to more people who might be a fit, and bring in new customers who enjoy the product like you do.

Get enough customers, and you can indeed live off those residuals like the Hollywood types do.

How many entrepreneurs does it take?

You may be surprised to learn that of the top bananas in the top companies, those with tens of thousands of people in their organizations and who have been working the business ten years or more, that in nearly ALL cases, they have fewer than four key people whose own organizations are responsible for 85-90% of the top banana's income. And in the majority of cases, those earning the fattest incomes, with tens of thousands of independent reps they've built up over the years, have just one or two entrepreneurs who are responsible for 85-90% of their income. Ask them.

Why do I tell you this?

To let you know that here, as in ANY endeavor, it does not take many people to make a difference.

Just one or two driven individuals will move thousands of others. Think John F. Kennedy in politics, Spielberg or Lucas in movies, Madonna or Jerry Seinfeld in entertainment, Rockefeller in oil/gas refining, Gates in computers, Edison in electricity, among others, Graham in Christianity, and on and on. Don't we all know a few names in different walks of life that that have impacted thousands?

If one knows to whom to present the business and how to do that, and if one of those special people gets caught up in it, that's when lives, spirits and fortunes change. It's one of the reasons the industry draws the millions of people it does. They're good people who want to change their lives with network marketing.

#4 There is no one 'best way' to reach out and find good matches for you, your products, services, or business.

Instead there are many, and they're all valuable because each reaching out method draws to it different people and uses your (or your team's) skills in different ways.

> *There are many different ways successful people have used to reach out to people, in order to make those introductions. Learn and practice 3-5 different proven methods so you're leveraged, and so you're a more interesting sponsor to good prospects. Your prospects will be people you know, people they know, and people you don't know (yet).*

Let no one tell you there is one best way to find those to whom you can make product or business introductions. Different people have done different things and been successful.[87]

There are probably 15 proven reaching out methods, all different, that have made people in the business wealthy. Some went to people they knew (warm market). Others NEVER went there, but went to people they didn't know (cold market).

---

[87] Kim Klaver 1998 pp 85-148

Some stood on street corners; others went door to door.[88]

There is no one best way for everyone. You may sometimes hear that the network marketing business is a business of 'duplication.' This is certainly not true as far as methods of reaching out are concerned.

Reaching out methods are personal choices. Not mandates from someone above. The ways you approach people depends on your preferences, personality, experience, and what turns you on.[89] Try different approaches. Invent others. See what feels right and good. Give yourself time to practice them and learn them.

---

[88] See http://mlm911.com/secrets2.html

[89] Kim Klaver (1998), pp. 85-148 for 13 methods of reaching out

#5. Say 'No' first.

> *The best defense is a good offense. This is the idea behind learning to say no first to anyone while you are trying to determine if you should take the time to make the introduction to your product, services or business.*

Often when people feel like they need to make a sale, begging sets in. Or high-pressure. This is very hard on relationships. Based on the dropout rates of 90% plus over the years, it's clear the most difficult part of the mission – 'Find people for whom it's the right thing to be doing now...' is to survive the process of sharing, showing and telling at all. For example, when they whine that they can't sell, agree. "Uh, you know, this is not something for you. I have another call. OK? Bye! Talk to you later!"

Selecting people to approach who are likely to be predisposed to your offer to begin with will help.

Learning to say no first is designed to keep those fragile egos whole, so entrepreneurs can keep on keeping on for another day. One day at a time.

#6. Do it in teams.

> *To help prevent fallout, for yourself or your team members, do all reaching out methods in teams or pairs.*

Teams help ensure new teammates don't melt down when they hear no or worse. Hearing a no all alone is the beginning of the end for most new people in the business.

Like exercising, going to church, or doing anything that it's easier not to do, pair up or team up so you all do the thing together. It works.

#7. Decide on your time and money budget.

How much time, money and honest effort will you put out to get your business off the ground and nurture it? It takes effort, energy, attitude, resources, and creativity to make any Plan B work, and you may not see results immediately.

As yourself: How much time and resources will you commit to building your business if you see no profits for the first 6-12 months? Building a business is kind of like having a baby. It takes a lot more effort AFTER those nine months of incubation then most new parents ever dreamed.

Most parents care for and nurture their children for their first 18 years. Or more.

We're not suggesting it will take THAT long. But building a business like this is a process that will require you to keep the faith many a time when no one else seems to have any, in you or in the venture. And that's why teams are so helpful. Sticking with others who also believe they can make a difference, supporting each other, helps bring out the best in everyone and helps everyone keep going.

Here's a story to hang on your wall.

How to plant and grow bamboo.

A bamboo farmer in Japan plants the bamboo shoots under the soil, and covers it with clay. It lies dormant for **four years.** *Then, as Mary Kay tells it:*

"Every morning, the farmer waters his potential crop, and at the end of the fourth year, the shoot finally breaks through the ground. Then, in only ninety days, the bamboo grows sixty feet!"

During that four-year period, the farmer doesn't even know for sure whether the plant is alive. But HE KEEPS THE FAITH AND DOESN'T ABANDON IT.[90]

#8. **Relax. Lighten up. Make introductions, not speeches. Use scripts that are simple and clear. Ask questions.**

---

[90] Mary Kay, pp 53-54.

> *When you have that chance to make the introduction to your service, product or business, remember the purpose: Show what you have to see if there might be a match with the other person. It's not to force a sale. Not pressing gives you a position of wonderful strength. And if there's a match, you have a sale.*

Remember what John Rockefeller related. To "solicit business" he wrote, "I made up my mind that I could do this best by simply introducing our firm, and not pressing for immediate consignments."[91]

And, he writes, "To our great surprise, business came in upon us so fast that we hardly knew how to take care of it."[92]

The personal touch and personal visit or call is what makes the network marketing business special. And not pressing on that first date gives

---

[91] John D. Rockefeller (1984), p. 49

[92] Ibid, p. 49

you a position of strength. What if you get the kind of results Mr. Rockefeller got, doing what he did?

17.
Tips to Get it in Your Lifetime

"If I do this, where am I going to get the right people? You know, the right people for the products and services, and the right entrepreneurs for the business? Where are they?"

In any Plan B, finding the right market is the first task. It might even be just one person who knows how to take you there.

Finding the right fit fast is especially important for a part-time beginner. Many people start with a few hours a day and don't have a lot of time to squeeze in between their regular job, their family life, and more.[93]

Here are some tips from those who have succeeded in skipping right over large numbers

---

[93] Maggie Jackson, May 19, 2002, *The New York Times*, p. 9

of wrong people straight to finding their right people.

Seeking predisposed markets

You now know that on average, 1%-8% of people out may be good fits for your product, service or business. That means 1-8 of 100. Untrained people try to talk to all 100 and mostly don't survive it, what with the pukies and all.

However, smart people first pinpoint those who are already inclined towards what they market. So they'll talk to perhaps 15-20 people to get the same one or two matches.

Smart people seek out and talk to **predisposed markets** - people who are already inclined to what they're offering.

Those are people who, by their actions and behaviors, show you that they're already leaning your way.

Dell made a list of all small businesses in his area he thought would be helped by a computer. He prioritized his list and starting calling to introduce his product and the service that came with it. Lauder went to beauty salons, because the women who went there were already inclined to try make-up and skin creams. Later she opened her own. John D. Rockefeller sought out those who were in businesses specifically "related" to his, and personally visited every one of them across two states in a horse drawn carriage.

How do you identify a predisposed market?

Pretend you represent a nutritional line.
Ask yourself: What *businesses/groups* in my area have customers/patients that are similar to mine? You know, like those tips Amazon.com gives to its customers when they buy a book: "People who bought book X also bought book(s) Y." Do you do what lots of people do right then? Yep. Buy one of those other books.

How about these as businesses predisposed to your products?

- MD's who include a focus on prevention, holistic medicine and nutrition. Aren't they already inclined your way? You don't have to sell them on the merits of prevention and nutrition. Check your local Yellow Pages.[94] Then you contact just those physicians and not the others.

- Alternative health practitioners. For example, chiropractors, massage therapists, acupuncturists, nutritionists, herbalists, etc. Aren't they all dealing in alternative health, and don't they all have clientele who are already inclined towards alternative solutions to health challenges, or who just believe in prevention?

- Associations or organizations of people who want to live longer, more energized lives or who want their health back (e.g. who got their wake-up call and are ready to mend their ways) cancer survivors, etc.

---

[94] Online national yellow pages at http://Verizonwuperpages.com)

What if you and a teammate systematically went to all the members of one such predisposed market in your area, one at a time, and you introduced yourselves and your product line to them? You can see if your products might be helpful to THEIR patients or clients.

If 1 in 15 or 20 say 'yes', there's a chance that one of those entrepreneurs (most of them are that) may either show your product line to their customers for you, or take a position themselves and become one of the entrepreneurs in your heap. They can then introduce the line to their own customers. Adding to both your heaps.

Regardless of the product or service you represent, begin by asking yourself certain questions.

> *Identifying your predisposed markets, one at a time. Ask these questions.*
>
> *What businesses or groups are inclined towards what I market? Who deals with similar kinds of clients to those I want? Who could benefit from this if they knew about it, and be ready to do something about it because they already are doing related kinds of things?*

With some brainstorming, you can come up with many folks who are already predisposed to what you market. Do the background work. Get prepared. That's what the greats did. Less barking up the wrong tree.

What about marketing to individuals?

Which individuals would be predisposed to nutritional or wellness supplements?

Anyone who demonstrates that they feel responsible for their own health. For example, people who:

work out already
eat organic;
read health publications;
visit alternative medical practitioners
attend weight loss groups
do yoga, etc.

Who is NOT so predisposed and likely to require therapy from you first?

The overweight brother-in-law who complains about his weight, but who does nothing about his eating habits, or makes little effort to learn about how to overcome the situation.

You think he needs it, hmm? But does *he*?

Decide: Do you want to do therapy or find the people who are predisposed towards your wares to begin with?

Even within a category, like nutritional products, seeking those who are predisposed will get you to the right people quicker. Say you market a concentrated wellness supplement that's in a spray form, or it might be a single concentrated drink. Instead of pills.

One predisposed group is people who take supplements in pill form already, and who'd consider an alternative to popping 5-15 pills a day. So ask for them. Here's a way.

Are you tired of choking down 13 pills each morning?

Who is likely to respond? Those who already take supplements, yes? And who might want something that comes in a more advanced form. No therapy required about the virtues of taking supplements to begin with. So you can have it in your lifetime.

There are lots of groups who are predisposed towards what you have. You have to think of who they might be, describe them, and ask for them.

Here's a formula we've used that helps you describe people who are inclined to whatever you market:

> **X is for people who blah blah, and blah blah, and who blah blah blah.**

The more specific the 'blah blah' is, the better.

Let's try one. Ask yourself, what is the edge an alternative telecom company like Excel or ACN has over the big three (AT&T, MCI and Sprint)?

Here's one. Each phone customer gets a personal rep who gives them over-the-top personal service. This is a significant edge, in my view, over the big three, because I value personal service.

So in the formula, we can describe this predisposed market:

An alternative phone service for people who want a phone company that offers over-the-top personal service; for people who have had it not being able to reach a live rep quickly from their phone company.

Nice, upscale, predisposed market.

Here are a few more examples describing people already inclined to certain products and services.

Here's an educational program for people who never realized they could save $5,000/year on their family income tax by just having a home based business, even if they didn't earn a dime in the business that year.

Finally. A home-cleaning-products line for those who are sensitive to the environment, who want to help save the earth or have little ones that eat off the floor.

These describe the people you seek for specific products or services. All who respond will be predisposed because that's whom you asked for.

And there are large organizations and like-minded people out there who already do related things that show you they're predisposed towards your wares.

For example, how about approaching accountants, financial and retirement planners for the tax saving program? Wouldn't some of their clients be interested?

Or, how about approaching people who recycle with that environmentally sensitive home-cleaning products line? Aren't they already predisposed to be kind to the environment? Ask for them in your approach:

Do you recycle?

You get the idea.

Reaching your predisposed markets: ***Describe that business, their clientele, or the individual.*** *Your specific description will be a related market for you. Then ask for them. There can be many related markets depending on what features of your goods, services or business you describe. Ask for then one at a time.*

How to find predisposed markets for your business opportunity.

Some people do the network marketing business because they love the products. Others love helping others. Still others seek the recognition, the leadership positions, the training and coaching, or they just love to inspire their teams and organizations.

People like this are all predisposed to the business. You know what to do next, right? Describe them (we just did a bit) and ask for them. For example:

Sales team leader wanted. Someone with experience in teaching, public speaking, motivational training, and owned business before.

There are many in direct sales and network marketing however, for whom the business is a means to an end. They want the income, immediate or long term, for other things. For example, those who suddenly realize the need to build up a retirement nest egg. Or those who want that extra income so they can stay home to home-school the kids. Perhaps they want to buy their parents a retirement home. Or they want to take the spouse or children to Paris at the drop of a hat – first class. And on and on.

Describe these kinds of people, specifically, one group at a time. These are your predisposed markets. And there are many more. Then ask for them. One at a time.

If the description is not specific, or if it's all-inclusive, everyone will respond. That may sound good until you remember only 1%-5% have what it takes or are ready to do what it takes to make it in a business of their own. Do you really want to talk to all of them?

Here's an old all-inclusive pitch:

Get big money, free time.

Who **doesn't** want more money and free time? That covers the panhandler on the corner to Bill Gates of Microsoft.

And that's exactly who the pitch attracts. Everyone. And the time wasting begins. Because the description doesn't say anyone has to do anything to get what's being offered. So many people hope it's something for nothing, or are surprised when they discover they'll have to put out honest effort and dollars.

Why not ask for those who are predisposed to what a Plan B can do for them in the first place?

Remember, one doesn't need that many key people or customers to make it in the business of direct sales and network marketing. 95% of all top bananas in the network marketing industry have between 1-4 key people who contribute 85%-90% of their giant incomes.

Here are some descriptions of predisposed folks, and a request for them to respond:

Are you worried about not having enough income for your retirement?

Do you want to end up like your parents, financially?

*Have you always wanted to **be** somebody?*

Do you think you can make a difference on our team?

Are you working 2+ jobs to make ends meet?

Do you have a Plan B?

See more examples elsewhere.[95]

Relationship Marketing. You are your own predisposed market member. Did you realize that?

Sometimes, the best place to start finding those right people is to seek out people who are like you in attitudes, beliefs, causes, history, or who can understand your pain because they've come from a

---

[95] Kim Klaver (1998), pp. 110-123
And http://www.harvardeditor.com
And http://www.mlm911.com.

similar place. Here's how to do that on your first 'date'. ☺

Most people know that creating rapport makes marketing easier. But that can take 5-10 contacts, some say. Here's a short cut for finding people who are predisposed towards certain issues the same way you are. Both for the product or service you market, and your business.

Ask yourself for the product or service, and the business: "Why do I buy the product or use the service?" And "Why am I really doing the business?"

Here are reasons people have given for using their nutritional or wellness products, for example.

    a. I've had migraine headaches for 10 years. After using this product for 6 weeks, they've largely subsided.
    b. I've had digestion problems for 11 years. After using this product for 30 days, I don't notice it anymore.

c. I've been overweight as long as I can remember, and tried lots of diets. I finally found something that has worked, and I've lost it and kept it off.

Who are the predisposed markets for each example? People who...what?

a. people who've suffered with migraines for 10 years
b. people who've suffered with digestion problems for years
c. people who've tried to lose weight and have been unsuccessful.

How big do you suppose each of these markets is across the country? And if any of these or similar people describe you, and you then get people like this on the phone, do you think you two will have an instant something to talk about that matters a lot to both of you? Is that the basis of a good relationship and an interesting discussion, at least? Will they all buy? ☹ But would you rather talk to people who are like you in important ways, at least?

You know the next step, yes? Ask for them. E.g. "Overweight? I lost 16 lbs in 11 weeks. Finally, safely. Call me and I'll tell you what I did."

If you market a weight management program, and this happened to you, would you want to talk to those who reply to this? Who do you think will respond to this ad? Is that who you want to talk to?

You can do the same for your business 'why'. Ask yourself: Why am I really doing this? What do I want to feel, experience or do that I can't do now? (Or couldn't do before if you have succeeded.)

Describe that specifically. And ask for those people. That's your predisposed market for growing your business with entrepreneurs. And there may be more than one, depending on how many things are driving you.

Say you have always wanted to travel throughout the exotic islands of the world. Or you've always pictured buying your retired parents a vacation home. How many other people are out there with that same goal? And who are ready to do something about it?

> Are these your only predisposed markets? There may be more. Likely there is one for each issue **you** take a strong stand on.

And when you talk to those who respond to your specific descriptions of what YOU want, or are sick of, you can have virtually instant rapport.

Describe it specifically and personally. You are your own predisposed market in this way for everything that matters to you. And ask for like minded people, one group at a time. So they can hear and recognize the call.

The goal in seeking and describing any predisposed market is to reduce the large numbers of unrelated cold and warm market members you have to talk to so you don't spend so much time with the wrong ones. One of the biggest regrets top bananas in the network marketing industry report is that they spent too much time with the wrong people.[96] You don't want to do that too, do you?

Last words.

As you learn about the network marketing business and meet people in it, you will no doubt speak to some who have failed. And who may have nothing good to say about the industry. Go ahead and talk to a few failures. But remember what Mary Kay advises:

"... [talking to people who have failed] may give you the wrong information. Failure may reflect the weaknesses of the individual rather than the business itself."[97]

And if you've decided to do the business, constantly practice saying no first, even if you desperately need the sale. It sends your brain a message. And, it also sends the other person's brain a message.

---

[96] Kim Klaver (1997), Audiotapes

[97] Mary Kay (1995), p. 142

"In the early days, when McDonald's was in no financial position to make demands on property owners, McDonald's Sonnenborn made them. He flatly rejected landowners who wanted escalator clauses or leases based on a percentage of sales. Those who watched his negotiating tactics marveled at his ability to put the property owner in a weaker position *by exercising the most critical of all negotiating skills: the ability to say "no deal'* whenever the other side's demands conflicted with his. By projecting such confidence, he convinced property owners and bankers that McDonald's had more financial substance than its balance sheet indicated. 'Harry negotiated as if he had a position of strength even when his position was really one of weakness.'"[98]

Singers know this too. Remember Madonna's big hit: "The Power of Good-bye"? And Alanis Morisette has a new one, called "Uninvited" an

---

[98] John F. Love (1986), pp. 161-162

enchanting song about a woman who uses rejection to regain the upper hand.[99]

Why do I stress this? Because we know that direct sales and network marketing is not for everyone. Like anything else that matters. Regardless of how much someone loves it, how much it has changed someone's life, when all is said and done, each person makes up his or her own mind. Despite our wishing that we could make it up for them. But this is how it should be. You wouldn't want someone forcing you, would you?

Here is my favorite example of a wonderful say-no-first attitude of someone who fell in love with his profession as a boy, and who's had a phenomenal impact on visionaries and thinkers around the world.

Not many people know that the inspiration for Star Wars, George Lucas' fabulous movie series, came from the life work of Joseph Campbell, legendary teacher and world-renowned mythologist.

---

[99] New York Times 6.10.02, B1

Campbell's monumental and awesome book, *'Hero with a Thousand Faces'* is perhaps the best known work on mythology to date and inspired much of the magic in the Star Wars saga.

Towards the end of his life Joseph Campbell spent numerous hours at Lucas' Skywalker Ranch in Marin County in California where acclaimed television journalist and interviewer Bill Moyers recorded Campbell's life's teachings including his thoughts on Star Wars, in hundreds of hours of conversations contained in a now legendary six-hour documentary *Joseph Campbell and The Power of Myth.*

However, it was in 1988 at the Museum of Natural History in New York, one of Joseph Campbell's most favorite places, that he and Bill Moyers sat together for a last conversation in Volume 6, *The Masks of Eternity.* He was close to 80.

At the end of their marathon sessions, Bill Moyers asked Campbell a bold question and here is Campbell's unbelievable answer:

> **Moyers:** *Why should we care about myths? What do they have to do with my life?*
> **Campbell:** *Go on and live your life as it is. It's a good life. YOU DON'T NEED THIS. I don't believe in being interested in subjects because it's said to be important and interesting.*
> *I believe in being caught up by it somehow or other.*
> *You may find that with the proper introduction this subject will catch you.*
> *And so, what can it do for you when it DOES catch you?[100]*

So I ask you: Why should you care about a Plan B?

Perhaps you don't need one. Maybe your life is a good life as it is.

---

[100] Joseph Campbell with Bill Moyers (1988), Audiotapes

But if it isn't good enough for you the way it is, and if you get caught up by the idea of something better, you've now been introduced to direct sales and network marketing.

What if you try it and it catches you? What if it works for you the way it has for thousands of others?

Can you picture what it can do for you when it does catch you? ☺

Epilogue

Dell is still #1 in PC sales today.

In describing Dell's quarterly earnings report posted 5.16.02, the *New York Times* reported that "Dell is gaining market share during the industry's difficult times." And most important:

"The Dell advantage lies not in technology, since all the largest PC makers rely in Intel's microprocessors and Microsoft's Windows operating systems. But Dell has perfected its direct-marketing model of selling to companies and consumers over the Internet or telephone, without resellers or retailers..." Dell's company reported "revenue of more than $8 billion in the quarter."[101] ☺

---

[101] Steve Lohr (May 2002), the *New York Times.*, p. C5

BIBLIOGRAPHY

AMERICAN HERITAGE DICTIONARY of the English
Language Fourth Edition. 2000. Boston, MA:
Houghton Mifflin Co.

ASH, Mary Kay. 1995. *Mary Kay: You can have it all:
Practical advice for doing well by doing good.*
Roseville, CA: Prima Publishing.

CAMPBELL, Joseph with MOYERS, Bill. 1993. *Joseph
Campbell and The Power of Myth with Bill
Moyers, Program Six – The Masks of Eternity.*
Minneapolis, MN: HighBridge Company. Audio
Cassettes.

CITRIN, James M. 2002. *Zoom: How 12 exceptional
companies are navigating the road to the next
economy.* New York, NY: Doubleday and
Company.

COLLINS, James and PORRAS, Jerry I. 1994. *Built to
Last: Successful habits of visionary companies.*
New York, NY: Harper Business.

EMERSON, Ralph Waldo. 1982. *Selected Essays.* "Self
Reliance". Middlesex, UK: Penguin Books, Ltd.

GATES, Bill. 1999. Business @ the Speed of Thought:
Using a digital nervous system. New York, NY:
Warner Books.

GODIN, Seth. 1999. Permission Marketing: Turning
strangers into friends and friends into customers.
New York, NY: Simon & Schuster.

BIBLIOGRAPHY

HILL, Napoleon. 1937/1988. Think and Grow Rich.
York, NY: Ballantine Books.

_____, 1993. *The Science of Personal Achievement.*
New York, NY: Simon & Schuster. Audio
Cassettes.

JACKSON, Maggie. May 19, 2002. *The New York
Times.* "Entrepreneurship is fun. Then there's the
day job." p. 9

KLAVER, Kim. 1996. *So you want to be a networker?*
Kansas City, MO: Max Out Productions. Audio
Cassette.

_____, 1997. *How to Build a Giant Heap with or without
your friends, family or neighbors.* Kansas City, MO: Max
Out Productions. Audio Cassettes.

_____, 1998. *The Truth. What it really takes to me it in
Network marketing.* Kansas City, MO: Max Out
Productions.

_____, 2000.. *Rules for the New New MLMer.* Kansas
City, MO: Max Out Productions.

KOEHN, Nancy. 2001. *Brand New: How Entrepreneurs
Earned Consumers' Trust from Wedgewood to
Dell.* Watertown, MA: Harvard Business School
Press.

LOHR, Steve. May 17, 2001. *The New York Times.*
"Dell's results match those of a year ago." p. C5

BIBLIOGRAPHY

LOVE, John F. 1986. *McDonald's: Behind the Arches*.
New York, NY: Bantam Books, Inc.

McCULLOUGH, David. 2001. *John Adams*. New York,
NY: Simon & Schuster.

MORISON, Samuel Eliot. 1983. *Christopher Columbus,
Mariner*. New York, NY: Meridien Books

ROCKEFELLER, John D. 1984. *Random Reminiscences
of Men and Events*. Tarrytown, NY: Sleepy
Hollow Press.

SCHWARTZ, John. April 4, 2002. *The New York Times*.
"Living on Internet Time in Another Age". p.E1

THE MIRACLES. 1960. *Shop Around*. Motown.

TRUMP, Donald and SCHWARTZ, Tony. 1987. Trump:
The Art of the Deal. New York, NY: Random
House